A Storied Singer

Recent Titles in Contributions to the Study of Popular Culture

A Storied Singer

Frank Sinatra as Literary Conceit

GILBERT L. GIGLIOTTI

Contributions to the Study of Popular Culture, Number 76

GREENWOOD PRESS
Westport, Connecticut • London

Library of Congress Cataloging-in-Publication Data

Gigliotti, Gilbert L., 1961–
 A storied singer : Frank Sinatra as literary conceit / Gilbert L. Gigliotti.
  p. cm.—(Contributions to the study of popular culture, ISSN 0198–9871 ; no. 76)
 Includes bibliographical references (p.) and index.
  ISBN 0–313–30973–6 (alk. paper)
  1. Sinatra, Frank, 1915—Criticism and interpretation. 2. Popular music—United States—History and criticism. 3. Popular culture. I. Title. II. Series.
 ML420.S565G44 2002
 782.42164′092—dc21   2001055606

British Library Cataloguing in Publication Data is available.

Library of Congress Catalog Card Number: 2001055606
ISBN: 0–313–30973–6
ISSN: 0198–9871

First published in 2002

Greenwood Press, 88 Post Road West, Westport, CT 06881
An imprint of Greenwood Publishing Group, Inc.
www.greenwood.com

Printed in the United States of America

The paper used in this book complies with the Permanent Paper Standard issued by the National Information Standards Organization (Z39.48–1984).

10 9 8 7 6 5 4 3 2

Copyright Acknowledgments

To the trio of ladies in my life:

my lovely wife, Martha,
"quin tibi sim iuvenis tuque puella mihi"
—Ausonius

and

our darling daughters, Cecilia and Celeste,
"Cherry pies ought to be you!"
—Cole Porter

Contents

Preface

Mud plate of Black Rock Desert passing, Frank Sinatra lamenting
distant years, old sad voic'd September'd recordings, and Beatles
crying Help! their voices woodling for tenderness.
　　　—Allen Ginsberg, "Beginning of a Poem of These States"

As the beat poet in this 1965 poem from *The Fall of America* suggests,
Frank Sinatra, long before his death on May 14, 1998, was ubiquitous,
an imposing and inescapable presence on the American landscape. His
music and films, his concerts and marriages (even his family, friends,
and enemies) had become a part of America's collective memory. His
life, in all its aspects, has been the regular subject of news reports in
both the tabloid and legitimate press as well as of miniseries, documen-
taries, and television movies. Even on NBC's youth-targeted *Saturday
Night Live* (*SNL*), the various incarnations of Sinatra were among the
most frequently portrayed of all the nonpolitical personalities.[1]

The public naturally thought they knew Sinatra because they had
heard and seen him so often. Consequently, Sinatra's work in both the
recording studio and on-screen has been understood through the of-

ten-exaggerated lens of his life. Much of his music, for example, is read almost exclusively as autobiography. Sinatra's 1951 recording of "I'm a Fool to Want You" has been accepted as the ultimate statement on his and actress Ava Gardner's doomed love. Conventional wisdom suggests that "I've Got the World on a String," recorded but a few months after he left Columbia Records,[2] trumpeted the dawn of the new, more confident and swinging Capitol Records Sinatra, and 1968's "My Way" apotheosized the singer as pop culture's preeminent survivor.[3] While such one-to-one correspondences are, of course, too facile and simplistic, they are nonetheless explicable. The identification of Sinatra's music with his life is the natural result of the two qualities that made the singer so popular (and the probable cause of his incredible longevity): first, the sense that he was singing directly to each member of the audience and, second, his ability to read a lyric. His interpretative talents simply made the audience forget that he, almost always, was singing someone else's words.[4]

Likewise, many of Sinatra's film roles—especially the more tough-minded and pugnacious characters from Danny Wilson and Angelo Maggio to *Pal Joey* Evans and *Tony Rome*—resonated with the public because of their apparent similarity to Sinatra's "real" personality, as reported by the press. Of course, to simply blame the press for these stories is simplistic since this image often was the result of Sinatra's own doing. Sinatra himself, after all, in begging producer Harry Cohn to let him audition for the role of Maggio in *From Here to Eternity*, had been quoted widely as saying, "It was written for me—for *me* and nobody else" (Shaw 169), and everyone always has accepted the resemblance. Nor did other public actions help to disprove the popular (mis?)conception because, in fact, he cursed and punched reporters, was photographed in the presence of underworld figures, and openly feuded with both American gaming commissions and Australia. In short, it became quite easy to blur the man, his myriad of images, and his art. And, due to his high profile, it did not matter who Francis Albert Sinatra was in real life; "Frank Sinatra" already had entered the public domain. The title of an off-Broadway revue that premiered in 2000 summed it up well: he had become our *Our Sinatra*.

From the early 1940s until now, this public presence has made Sinatra a marketer's dream. His name and image have been used to sell everything from Michelob beer and rechargeable radios to Gap khaki trousers,[5] Atlantic City,[6] and Cadillacs[7]—not to mention his own (and others') records, movies, casinos, and restaurants. To the populace at large, Frank Sinatra clearly signified something, but what? The answer, of course, depended upon the year and intended audience.[8]

In 1964, for example, Connie Francis recorded and released *A New Kind of Connie* for MGM Records. Into the album's first cut, the jazz standard "Will You Still Be Mine," she interpolates Sinatra's name into the litany of impossible, or at least hard-to-imagine, events used to mark the length of her man's love for her. Along with the viability of lovers no longer meeting and the Hudson River's no longer being romantic, Sinatra's gaining weight is offered as a point in time too remote to imagine. It seemed to make no difference that by 1964, though far from stout, the skinny kid from New Jersey had long outgrown joking references to his thinness that persisted throughout the first decade of his fame. Connie, as the album's title makes clear, was courting a new kind of record buyer, not the young "Where the Boys Are" crowd, but an older, more sophisticated audience[9] who would appreciate liner notes by veteran songwriter Jimmy McHugh. McHugh's own invocation of "Frank Sinatra" not once, but twice, in the space of four short paragraphs only further emphasizes the marketing clout the name had.

Even musicians from very different times and places tend to see themselves in relation to the man. In the 1980s, the British band "Frankie Goes to Hollywood" took their name from a 1940s headline announcing Sinatra's move into movies; while a group formed in Irvine, Scotland, around 1987 simultaneously declared their fealty to and distance from the classic pop tradition with their sardonic name, "Trashcan Sinatras."[10] But Sinatra was not only seen as a benchmark for younger musicians because of his music; his well-documented lifestyle also meant much to them. According to Robbie Robertson in the 1978 Martin Scorsese documentary *The Last Waltz*, when Ronnie Hawkins invited Robertson to join his band, "The Hawks," the veteran knowingly offered this bit of added incentive, "Well, son, you won't make much money, but you'll get more pussy than Frank Sinatra." In 1995, the heavy metal band Victim's Family released "Sinatra Mantra," which skewers Sinatra as a loathed authority figure even as it demonstrates a thorough knowledge of the details of the entertainer's life and career, from Ava and the mob to his battles with the press and his line of Italian foods. And, in 2000, rapper Craig Mach sampled "High Hopes" for his song "Wooden Horse."

In film, Sinatra's diverse but pervasive presence is also inescapable.[11] In Walt Disney's animated version of "Casey at the Bat," from the 1946 "package feature" *Make Mine Music*, for example, Casey's status as a popular figure over whom all the girls swoon makes him 1902's version of Sinatra. In John Sayles's *Baby, It's You* (1983), Vincent Spano's character of "The Shiek" declares that only two people in history have mattered: Jesus Christ and Frank Sinatra. The quest of "Pondo Sinatra" to lose his virginity in David Beaird's 1984 Canadian coming-of-age comedy, *The Party Animal*, co-opts both of Sinatra's more recognizable erotic film personae: the naïf of *Anchors Aweigh* and *On the Town*, as well as the experienced ladies' man of *Pal Joey* and the Rat Pack movies. In Barry Levinson's *Good Morning, Vietnam* (1987), only "certain ballads by Frank Sinatra" are deemed acceptable to the officer in charge of official broadcasts, played by Bruno Kirby.[12] Lieutenant Hauk's qualification of Sinatra's music, of course, implies that he senses in some Sinatra recordings the same dangers he fears in the rock music Robin Williams's Adrian Cronauer really wants to air.[13] And "Frankie," the heroine and namesake of Sinatra in writer-director Tiffanie DeBartolo's *Dream of an Insomniac* (1998), knows that, in David, she finally has met Mr. Right when his blue eyes literally light up the screen. Of course, one cannot overlook Mel Brooks's send-up of the Sinatraesque style in his performance of the title song of his 1977 comic homage to Hitchcock, *High Anxiety*.

Not infrequently Sinatra transcends mere mention or allusion, and his presence can permeate a film. The explosive and, at times, unsophisticated culture clash of the Italian Americans and African Americans in Spike Lee's 1989 *Do the Right Thing* is crystallized in this exchange between Lee's Mookie and John Turturro's Pino:

> You know, Pino, fuck you, fuck your fuckin' pizzeria, and fuck Frank Sinatra.
>
> Well, fuck you, too, and fuck Michael Jackson.

Sparked by "Buggin' Out's" vehement objection to having only Italian Americans on the "Wall of Fame" in Sal's Famous Pizzeria, the racial tensions of the entire Bedford-Stuyvesant neighborhood come to center upon the pictures of celebrities and sports stars such as Joe DiMaggio, Dean Martin, Liza Minnelli, Robert DeNiro, and Al Pacino. But it is the picture of a young Francis Albert Sinatra that takes center stage. Aside from its being part of the first pair (together with DiMaggio) shown on the wall by director Lee and the one on which the camera finally lingers as the restaurant goes up in flames, Sinatra's picture hangs at the booth used most frequently throughout the film. Repeatedly, therefore, Sinatra's young face appears on screen. Given the film's keen sense of the countercurrents that run through the history of race in the United States from every perspective, it is clear that the director's choice of Sinatra was not simplistic. It seems apparent that Lee recognized Sinatra's place—not only in the Italo-American community, but also in the civil rights movement, epitomized by his 1945 short feature on racial and religious tolerance, *The House I Live In*.[14] In Sinatra, therefore, Lee offers his audience (as he does much more prominently with Martin Luther King, Jr. and Malcolm X) an icon with a myriad of significant, and mixed, connotations by putting yet another face on the complicated issue of race in American society.

In Doug Liman's *Swingers*, despite a soundtrack that boasts songs by Dean Martin, Tony Bennett, Roger Miller, and Bobby Darin (though none by Hoboken's favorite son), it is Frank's presence alone that dominates the action—much the way his picture (albeit this time a cracked one) once again hangs in one of the underground clubs the gang frequents. After all, the schedules of these Rat Pack wannabes revolve around "Sinatra Night" at the Lava Lounge and parties in honor of Sinatra's birthday. But just like Frank's broken picture, their image of Sinatra's erotic meaning needs fixing, for sexual conquest in the film leads not to intimacy but to emptiness. The movie's only truly intimate act between a man and a woman is the swing dance in which John Favreau's Mike and Heather Graham's Lorraine engage toward the end of the film. Unlike the need of Mike's male buddies, Trent and Sue, to detail and refine the rules that govern sexual interaction and necessarily prevent sincere relationships, Mike and Lorraine's affection for one another is honest, healthy, and quite sexy. In fact, it is not hard to imagine that screenwriter/star Favreau had in mind Sinatra's recording of Sammy Cahn's "Come Dance with Me" with its clear equivalence of dancing and intercourse.

As Trent and Sue observe the dance with an increasingly less casual, more emotional eye, even these experienced swingers, now almost in tears, recognize that something different, something truly erotic, is happening; what begins as mere scorekeeping evolves into an awareness of an absence in their own lives. For only when Mike and Lorraine remain true to the romantic possibilities of Sinatra—as opposed to the merely sexual ones upon which their friends fixate—can love enter their lives.

In the public consciousness, therefore, there are any number of fictional, metaphorical, lyrical, and satirical Sinatras, and it is these creations in which the present study is interested. *A Storied Singer* examines the diverse ways in which writers of song, fiction, drama, and poetry have created and employed the several personas of Frank Sinatra as a literary construct in their texts.

The first part, "Self-Portraits," investigates the image of Sinatra that he and his many collaborators created over the course of his career. The studies in this section include, among others, an analysis of the poems that served as the basis for Sinatra's 1956 orchestral project, *Tone Poems of Color*. Part I also offers close readings of songs and song suites composed especially for Sinatra: the many lyrics of Sammy Cahn, 1969's *Watertown* (*A Love Story*), and 1979's *The Future* by Gordon Jenkins.

Deriving its title from a Rickie Lee Jones lyric, the second part, " 'Sad-Eyed Sinatras' in Song and Story," focuses on how quickly and consistently other writers of diverse backgrounds and genres have co-opted the Sinatra image to their own, quite disparate, ends. This section explores the metaphorical use of Sinatra in popular music (from the 1940s to 2001) and several literary works, including: Raul Nuñez's 1984 Spanish novella, *Sinatra*, translated into English as *The Lonely Hearts Club*; Bernard Kops's 1991 British drama, *Playing Sinatra*; Neil A. Shurley's 1996 short story, "Commandments"; and Sam Kashner's 1999 novel, *Sinatraland*.

At this point, I would like to caution the reader to abandon any conception of *A Storied Singer* as a biographical study of Sinatra. While primarily chronological, it focuses upon artistic and metaphorical repesentations of Sinatra rather than the historical details of his life and career. The several, and often conflicting, Sinatras who will appear throughout the remainder of this text are the creations of writers who have invoked the images and myths surrounding the celebrity known as "Frank Sinatra." This interpretative distance is as critical as it is vast. Thus, the links between Sinatra and incestuous British siblings or a down-on-his-luck Spanish hotel desk clerk are imaginative associations and metaphorical connections that say more about what Sinatra has meant to authors and audiences than about the Francis Albert Sinatra born in Hoboken, New Jersey, in 1915. Naturally, the historical Sinatra enters into this equation, but only as another variable—not the defining element or determining factor. Just as artists' understandings of their own works become readings no more or less valid than the interpretations of critics and scholars, the "real" Sinatra and those who knew him have only limited say in how the public will read him in the future. For better or worse, Frank Sinatra belongs to everyone now.

ACKNOWLEDGMENTS

I am, of course, hopelessly indebted to many. First of all, my thanks go out to all the writers, poets, novelists, lyricists, and playwrights, whose words this book explores. I also would like to thank Central Connecticut State University (CCSU) for its financial commitment to this project in the form of a sabbatical leave and travel expenses. I also thank the faculty, staff, and alumni of the English Department at CCSU, past and present (chiefly, Loftus Jestin, Stuart Barnett, Paul Beeching, Tony Cannella, Min Fang, Susan Gilmore, Cindy Guertin, Tom Hazuka, Jane Hikel, Allan Hirsch, Michael Manson, Mary Anne Nunn, Ken Parille, Jerry Tullai, Bill Weinberger, Jill Weinberger, and Phyllis Vinci) for all of their support—factual, critical, and moral. I especially acknowledge the three small but sincere English 288 summer classes (Scott Attenello, Justin Cannon, Margaret and Stephen Grzybowski, Colleen Hannah, Lisa Phillipo, and Angela Tosca in 1999; Robert Brzozowski, Lindsay Drzwecki, Stacey Ehlert, Tanya Hodder, Joe Karas, David LaGamba, and Carease Mitchell in 2000; and Sergio Guerrera, Cameron Lane, Michele Mallon, Mitchell Sinatra, Scott Steinberg, Deidre Updegraff, Rebecca Uricchio, and Michael Wright in 2001) who brought their energy and excitement to the reading of many of the works discussed in these pages. Recognition also is due to others: CCSU colleagues Thom Delventhal, Josh Perlstein, Domenic Forcella, Heather Munro Prescott, Joseph McKeon, Felton Best, George Muirhead, and President Richard Judd; the student staff of WFCS 107.7 FM New Britain/Hartford, who since 1993 have allowed me the weekly opportunity to showcase all things Sinatra on "Frank, Gil, and Friends"; and the internet discussion groups to which I have belonged over the years ("The Voice" and Temple lists) for their daily inspiration, information, and the reminder that Sinatra will never die. I also acknowledge my debt to people who have supplied me with the odd detail and/or encouraging word during the course of my research: among many others, Beverly Elander, Rick Apt, Ed O'Brien, Carolyn Saunders, Lisa Leone, Michael Wright, Andrew Gladwin, Richard Choi, Gregory Besharah, Bill Modic, John Boonstra (for *King Corso*), Amy Wergeles, Coleen Toews, and Clifton Wiens.

I would be quite remiss if I did not offer my heartfelt gratitude to all the dear friends (you know who you are) who have tolerated and often abetted my "Sinatraholism" over the years. Special thanks are also due my loving family, particularly my parents, who've been rolling their eyes about this for two decades. Of course, many thanks are due Marcia Goldstein, Eric Levy and his predecessor, Pamela St. Clair, Betty Pessagno, Fran Lyon, and the editorial staff at Greenwood Press for their invaluable assistance and considerable patience.

NOTES

1. The two most famous impersonations were by Joe Piscopo and the late Phil Hartman.

2. The very first song Sinatra recorded at Capitol was the decidedly forgettable "Lean Baby," lyrically no more promising than the so-called nadir of Sinatra's Columbia period, "Mama Will Bark." Perhaps the only new development is the fact that the joke about thinness, a key characteristic in Sinatra's image in the 1940s, is not about *his* slenderness; it concerns the woman's.

3. It tends to be overlooked, in light of the song's pervasiveness since the 1970s, that this anthem to survival was recorded *before* his 1971 retirement, when Sinatra obviously thought that the end had arrived.

4. According to Silva, Sinatra would receive writing credit on seven songs in his career: "This Love of Mine" (1941), "Sheila" (1950), "Peachtree Street" (1950), "Take My Love" (1950), "I'm a Fool to Want You" (1951), "Mistletoe and Holly" (1957), and "Mr. Success" (1958).

5. Unlike similar images of Miles Davis and James Dean, Sinatra's advertisement for the Gap, "Frank Sinatra Wore Khakis," marked the first time the ad campaign had used the image of a person still living.

6. Sinatra's 1988 recording of the Paul Anka composition, "Leave It All to Me," was used to promote the New Jersey town as a vacation destination.

7. Right after Sinatra's death in May 1998, Cadillac ran full-page advertisements with a black-and-white picture of a vintage car with blue headlights and the caption "It's been a great ride."

8. The advertising copy on the back of the 1956 *Songs for Swingin' Lovers* makes precisely this point by offering a litany of the audiences for whom Sinatra performed during his recording and film career: "for teenagers . . . for adventure-loving moviegoers . . . for sad romantics . . . for observers of the social scene . . . and now for swingin' lovers."

9. Contrast Francis's use with Anita O'Day's 1945 reference in her patriotic "I Want a Grown Up Man," which pits matinee idols Sinatra, Victor Mature, and Cary Grant against the more mature, and hence more attractive, Uncle Sam.

10. Sinatra has influenced the naming of not a few bands. The Spinatras, a metal band, for example, obviously followed the recommendation of *The Simpsons'* Principal Skinner by settling on a name "that's witty at first but seems less funny each time you hear it," while The Skanatras are exactly what they sound like: a ska band that plays Sinatra songs. And the British trio, Danny Wilson, co-opted the title of a fairly obscure Sinatra film, *Meet Danny Wilson*, for its 1987 debut album.

11. Sinatra's film cameos over the years, in everything from *Till the Clouds Roll By* (1946) and *Around the World in 80 Days* (1956) to *The Road to Hong Kong* (1962) and *Cannonball Run II* (1983) also testify to the hold that Sinatra continued to have on the public imagination throughout his long career.

12. Sinatra clearly holds a prominent place in Barry Levinson's view of American culture (at least as seen from his native Baltimore). In his 1982 film, *Diner*, there is the classic scene in which the friends debate who offers the better "make out" music: Johnny Mathis or Sinatra, as well as the young character in his 1999 film, *Liberty Heights*, who, out of respect for the singer, repeatedly refuses to leave a car if a Sinatra song is playing on the radio.

13. While admittedly both *Good Morning, Vietnam* and *Baby, It's You* are period pieces set in the early 1960s and therefore demand cultural references to that particular era, that the writers chose to use Sinatra in the ways they did is nonetheless significant. In fact, that Sinatra still possessed enough cultural currency to be comprehensible to a 1980s audience is perhaps most telling of all.

Even as late as 1995, Sinatra was still an unavoidable presence on television—without appearing himself. The October 10, 1995, episode of NBC's *Frasier*, "Martin Does It His Way," focused upon a song the psychiatrist's father had begun writing for the singer decades before. On two different series, there also were a pair of characters with the last name Sinatra: "Sammy Sinatra" on CBS's *The Bonnie Hunt Show* and "Kelly Sinatra" on Showtime's *Sherman Oaks*, suggesting once again that the name was not inconsequential. Unlike a character named "Sammy Bennett" or "Kelly Crosby," the Sinatra name draws attention to itself the way few other names in popular culture do.

The late 1990s brought *The Sopranos*, the mob-as-suburban-family series on HBO, with its familiar and familial references to "Francis Albert" and even a cameo appearance by Frank, Jr.

14. As part of this 1945 personal crusade for tolerance, Sinatra also penned an essay, "What's This about Races?," for the September 17 issue of *Scholastic Magazine* and on November 1, he appeared at a high school in Gary, Indiana, where racial tensions were running high (Kuntz and Kuntz 42, Nancy Sinatra 69).

The Man in Many Looking Glasses: From an Obscene Gerund to a *Pas de Deux*

The pair of Frank Sinatras conceived by Garry Trudeau and Twyla Tharp, both the petty bullying and the emotional physicality, are vividly dramatic and quite believable, and it is in the credibility of both images that the strength of the crass thug of "Doonesbury" and the passionate *danseur* of *Sinatra Suite* lie. Of course, the pertinent issue for any investigation into the representations of perhaps the single most significant pop cultural figure of the twentieth century is not which is truer or which more accurately captures the man, Francis Albert Sinatra (1915–1998). The important point is that the seemingly contradictory figures have become ingrained in the public imagination and coexist. Both, in short, are true . . . whether the facts support them or not. That is the beauty and danger of artistic creation: the ability to make even the most remarkable notion, character, or situation seem plausible. Nor can it be denied that Sinatra's continuing hold on the popular imagination is, in no small part, indebted to the raw power of such characters as depicted in media as disparate as comic strips and ballet.

Sinatra's legendary status, it must be remembered, is not only about his obvious talent, musical and dramatic; his storied life was not built only upon his own artistic and philanthropic achievements, though those elements must not be dismissed or ignored. His legacy, however, does include, and should not be separated from, the stories (real and imagined) that arose around him, both with his cooperation and independently of him. In short, along with so many other things, Sinatra is an obnoxious cartoon and also a suave and athletic ballet dancer. While the juxtaposition of images may sometimes have a jarring effect, the resulting picture, though quite messy, can be richer and more satisfying than any single biography of the man himself. For while Trudeau's strips may have angered many on account of the acerbity of the satire, and Tharp's choreography may have lionized his music as the epitome of a tragic romanticism, both capture his compelling force, his inability to be ignored. And that is the one Sinatra characteristic that cannot be denied.

In the series of "Doonesbury" comic strips on Sinatra from 1985, the initial strength of the satire rests on the journalistic details: the direct quotations and the photographs. For fans of Sinatra, it would have been bad enough that in the strips Trudeau portrays Sinatra as arrogant, imperious, short-tempered, and petty, everything they had always heard and read about Sinatra but have been able to overlook, dismiss, or discount because of the artistry of his performances. "Okay," they say, "maybe he behaved like a real jerk sometimes, but listen to *Only the Lonely* or *Moonlight Sinatra*. Watch *On the Town* or *The Manchurian Candidate*. That's what should matter: the work." Nevertheless, Trudeau's critique hits hard; the strips all but scream, "How could anyone, much less the United States of America or an institution of higher education, grant any honor to a man who consorts with hoodlums?" The answer, for Trudeau, is mind-numbingly obvious, although, in the spirit of all political cartoonists, he also firmly believes that if readers choose to disagree with his viewpoint, the cartoon should at least provoke as visceral a response as possible from them. And that it does. Even so, the fan must question why Trudeau had to include the precise language of the honorary degree from the Stevens Institute and the Medal of Freedom award, as well as actual photographs of Frank with known mobsters.

The accusations in the strips of mob affiliation and fraternization (or, at the very least, a dangerous proximity) were hardly new, of course. The stories of Mafia connections dated back at least to the late 1940s, and the apocryphal tale of some underworld help in releasing Sinatra from his contract with band leader Tommy Dorsey went all the way back to 1942. Nor were accounts of Sinatra's anger hardly infrequent. Didn't he, long before Sean Penn was even born, punch out columnist Lee Mortimer? Didn't Sinatra feud with the entire CONTINENT of

Australia? Nevertheless, couldn't the cartoonist simply keep Sinatra "offscreen" with only the ugly words visible? Did he need to include the conclusion of Ronald Reagan's May 23, 1985, introduction of Sinatra, with the inevitable cliché, "and one who truly did it his way," and a 1976 photograph of Sinatra with Don Carlo Gambino, Jimmy "The Weasel" Fratianno, et al. Could it not have been more fictional, more cartoonish, more make-believe?

That has never been the way of "Doonesbury." Its combination of an outlandishly comic vision and often-harsh political and social commentary helped change the way the "comics" were viewed. For several years, some newspapers even have refused to run the strip on the comics page, deeming it necessary to place it on the op-ed page (or somewhere else) to make it clear that it is not another "Beetle Bailey," "Hi and Lois," or "Family Circus."[1] Ironically, the comics pages are filled increasingly with strips as political and outspoken as "Doonesbury," all without suffering the fate of being shipped off to another section of the daily paper or being labeled as "commentary by."

Trudeau, like all political cartoonists, depends upon a readership readily familiar with the events and people he lampoons, and the well-documented life of Sinatra offered him plenty of fodder for his strips. Much always has been made in the press about both the singer's successes and his failings, his highs and lows. Nineteen eighty-five was no different: along with the Medal of Freedom and the honorary doctorate came the news of boorish behavior, with Sinatra trying to get a dealer fired from the Golden Nugget in Atlantic City. Trudeau took advantage of the concurrence of these events, and once he had introduced the series with the broadside attack of the quotations and pictures, a more subtle, fanciful, and successful depiction of Sinatra in the casino could don the feeling of authenticity, even as it obviously exaggerates the circumstances.

It is quite evident that Trudeau understood (and took advantage of) Sinatra's extravagant marquee value by his choice of a line from one of the five four-panel Sinatra strips as the title of his 1986 collection, *"That's Doctor Sinatra, You Little Bimbo."* As but one very small part of the collection, the strip's being raised to an almost thematic significance for the anthology is misleading at best. The collection is anything but a sustained satire of Sinatra. Other plot lines, such as Boopsie's B-movie career, Lacey Davenport's confrontation of racism in Palm Springs, or even Marcia's "celebration of her singularity," are sustained far longer and are far more of-the-moment than the Sinatra strips. Trudeau knew that the Sinatra name itself would sell books, however, and so he placed it (and Sinatra's mob group shot) on his cover. He even parodies the usually favorable reviewers' blurbs on the back cover, by offering condemnations of the Sinatra strips as "tasteless and unfair," "off base," "dreadful," and "funny as a tumor," from Congressman Joseph J. DioGuardia, Joe Piscopo,[2] Angie Dickinson, and even Sinatra himself. As both his target and his pitchman, Sinatra served Trudeau very well, and Trudeau obviously appreciated Sinatra's uniqueness.

Uncharacteristically, the cartoonist utilizes no metonymy in his portrayal of Sinatra, and, as unlikely as this may sound, this artistic decision suggests an appreciation of Sinatra's stature. Very often, for example, Trudeau depicts well-known figures symbolically, with an image or object that reflects some particularly significant aspect of their personality or position. He denotes presidents (such as Reagan or Clinton), for example, with the image of the White House, a common metaphorical substitution utilized by the press: "The White House today announced."[3] In fact, Trudeau utilizes this exact metonymy in the strips about the Medal of Freedom. The single image in the first three panels is of the front of the White House with the conversation of (or proclamation by) the president written directly above the structure.

Trudeau offers no such metonymic image to represent Sinatra, however; if it is not the reproduction of a photograph, he keeps him entirely out of view. While one could simply argue that the cartoonist thought the energy invested in drawing Sinatra would not offer a good enough comic return, there are other ways to read it. On the one hand, the depiction of a man of seventy would most probably not portray accurately the force that Sinatra still commanded in 1985. On the other hand, it might be suggested that, given Sinatra's multifaceted nature as a public figure, no single image could convey him adequately. Somehow, characterizing him as a singer, actor, or even temperamental and pampered star inevitably would leave many in the audience wondering exactly whom he was satirizing. The many Sinatras that people carry with them—be it the slender, bow-tied boy with a remarkable voice, the swinging Rat Packer, or the portly gentleman in evening clothes—prevented Trudeau from comically reducing him to any single emblem. And that implies much about Sinatra. After all, the comic shorthand Trudeau employs for the contentious former Speaker of the House, Newt Gingrich (a bomb with a lit fuse), and the "lightweight" former vice president, Dan Quayle (a feather), pictorially supports his satiric contention that those particular characteristics sum them up completely. While he wants to be funny, and the genre demands concision, most importantly the metonymies must convey Trudeau's point of view. In the case of his depiction of Sinatra, Trudeau was forced, as it were, to represent Sinatra either photographically or not at all, and, as a result, the cartoonist pays him at least a little tribute. Too big to limit, Sinatra demanded individual treatment.

Trudeau's special handling of Sinatra also includes the comic deletion of the entertainer's cursing of the dealer. As he gets more and more frustrated at her refusal to deal the cards without shuffling (in violation of casino rules), he screams: "Get me your (obscene gerund) BOSS, you little (anatomically explicit epithet)!" To which she responds to herself, "Obscene gerund?" Here, of course, Trudeau satirically castigates Sinatra for (1) thinking himself above the rules; (2) being rude; and (3) being crude. The success of the strip's satire, however, stems from his ability to amuse even as he means to offend his readers with Sinatra's behavior. If the readers are not offended at least a bit by the language they themselves must use to fill in the circumlocutions, he has failed in his caricature; if people find it only funny but see nothing inappropriate, his point has missed its mark. At the same time, he also has not succeeded if the crudity of the cartoon prevents his audience from seeing the humor of its execution. The obscene gerund punch line diffuses the issue by depicting the exchange through a mocking self-censorship that only accentuates the line of decency Sinatra had crossed. Thus, not only by having his characters speak in vulgar periphrasis but also having other characters hear it that way, Trudeau fully exploits the strip's comic possibilities—both in terms of its humor and its genre. In other words, the artist has fully realized the cartoon Sinatra by characterizing him in ways only available to the comic strip form. Perhaps it is not the real Sinatra, but he is as real as Mike Doonesbury, Zonker, Honey, or Duke, and that is no small achievement.

A similarly successful attempt to capture Sinatra in a decidedly different medium than we are accustomed to seeing the singer is Twyla Tharp's 1984 balletic incarnation of him in her *Sinatra Suite*. Choreographed especially for Mikhail Baryshnikov, Tharp revisited *Nine Sinatra Songs*, her 1982 dance for seven couples whose "individual duets combine to play out the stages of any relationship" (Tharp 274). The briefer, more compact *Suite* was performed on the Russian dancer's PBS television special, "Baryshnikov by Tharp," broadcast on October 5, 1984, and then officially premiered on December 9 at the Kennedy Center for the Performing Arts in Washington, D.C. The ballet, danced by Baryshnikov and Elaine Kudo to a medley of five of Sinatra's most popular hits—("Strangers in the Night," "All the Way," "That's Life," "My Way," and "One for My Baby (and One More for the

Road)"—traces what Baryshnikov refers to in the television introduction as "the theme of most ballets . . . love won and love lost."

The ballet opens with the dancers enacting the love-at-first-sight scenario specifically described in "Strangers." The man and woman, attired in evening clothes designed by Oscar de la Renta, see each other from across a crowded room and immediately leave hand in hand under a starlit sky. Once outside, the couple's movements are grand and sweep across the entire stage. Although Tharp's vigorous choreography, a mixture of classical ballet and modern dance movements, captures the elation and vitality of new love, it also is apparent that the love in which they are reveling is, at this early stage, a bit anonymous because the lovers rarely look at each other. It is as if they are so caught up in the power of the emotion of the moment that the identity of the partner is less important than the activities and energy they share. Nonetheless, the emotions they experience are very real.

By the second song, the initial bursts of energy are gone, but in their place are movements of a much more intimate and risky nature. Almost continually face-to-face, Baryshnikov and Kudo dance with a mature eroticism, displayed in the closeness and intricacy of the movements. The trust they have in each other only heightens the intimacy and, as a result, quite powerfully reveals the passionate commitment of their going "All the Way," even despite the vulnerability and uncertainty displayed in the Sammy Cahn lyric.

The road to trouble begins with the sounds of the raucous keyboard prelude of "That's Life." Baryshnikov has taken off his tuxedo jacket and is chewing gum as a rougher physicality and freneticism dominates the dancers' movements. Inspired by the "apache . . . a dance from the seaport of Marseilles, where the guy . . . hurls his partner about, [and which] comes disturbingly close to cruelty" (Tharp 276), Tharp's choreography alternates between the couple's pulling, pushing, caressing, and shaking each other. At one point, Baryshnikov even drags Kudo across the stage. For all the violence, however, the attraction and trust they share have not disappeared entirely, as is evident from the conclusion of this segment of the ballet. To the strains of the climactic ending of the song, from the opposite end of the stage, Kudo runs headlong toward a Baryshnikov who seems utterly unaware of her approach. She leaps into the air just as he turns toward her, and she flies forcefully into his arms. Back together after a turbulent period, she helps him on with his jacket once again.

The end of the affair is near, however, as the next song, "My Way," declares in its opening line. Consequently, the choreography takes on a decidedly formal feel and the lovers seem distant . . . even as they continue their waltz-like *pas de deux*. And when the song concludes, she departs the stage, leaving him completely alone.

The final song, "One for My Baby," brings the suite full circle by concluding with a selection as readily dramatized as "Strangers in the Night." Baryshnikov, tie loosened and in his shirtsleeves, stumbles about intoxicated, depressed, and a bit pugnacious until he finally wanders offstage as the tinkling piano music fades to silence. With his jacket over his shoulder, he poignantly echoes the late-night loneliness depicted on the covers for such albums as *In the Wee Small Hours* (1955) and *The Point of No Return* (1961).

While both the opening and closing numbers are almost too obvious in their inclusion, the complete reinvention of the third and fourth songs in the suite makes the entire concept in many ways more compelling. Since both "That's Life" and "My Way" deal more generally with the notions of struggle and survival, neither song is traditionally understood as a love ballad. Tharp's placing them within the erotic context of her ballet, however, sheds a new, and much-needed, light on the pair of songs. Consequently, instead of being overplayed anthems to staying power and an almost obstinate pride, the songs' more painful undercurrents are examined. The solitary but self-assured search for identity normally identified in "That's Life," for instance, comes instead to reflect their many conflicting attempts to find happiness together, even as the draining push and pull of the choreography dramatizes the stresses and strains that will finally drive them apart. Meanwhile, within the context of a dying love, the self-congratulatory dimension of "My Way" takes on an almost penitential tone, as the now lonely man must confront directly the results of doing it his way.

Significantly, this reinterpretation of "My Way" differs drastically even from Tharp's own use of it in *Nine Sinatra Songs*, where she happily suggests that "for a couple to work it needs to be a successful joining of two individual 'my ways'" (Tharp 275).[4] Unlike the exuberant pitches and aerial work of that dance, the sedate formality and unhappy ending of the song in *Sinatra Suite* offers no such illusion of happiness. This less optimistic view of romance in *Sinatra Suite* only testifies to Tharp's suspicions of the remarkable success the earlier ballet enjoyed. As she writes in her 1992 autobiography, *When Push Comes to Shove*: "I did have to wonder, though, if the silent story of enduring relationships I told was not, just like the nineteenth-century ballets, a fairy tale" (277). Everything in her experience told her that love was not like what she had depicted in *Nine Sinatra Songs*, so in *Sinatra Suite* she simply aimed at being more honest.

By altering her audience's understanding of even very familiar music, Tharp prepares them for an original Sinatra, one defined not only by words or music but motion. Still possessing the lover's (and loser's) soul, Sinatra now also has a dancer's body, and the choreography translates the tenderness and toughness exposed in his vocal inflections into action. The word, as it were, becomes flesh.

Just as Garry Trudeau sketched "ol' blue eyes" as a viable, if unsympathetic, portrait, so Tharp choreographed a kinetic voice: familiarly elegant, romantic, and, at times, combative, but for the first time personified in a tautly explosive corporeality, the physical embodiment of love and heartbreak. In the end, these two very different Sinatras betray a single truth—the power of art to shape an authentic reality without regret. In "Doonesbury" and *Sinatra Suite*, an audience may not find the historical Sinatra, but there is an authenticity in them nonetheless, for the compelling vitality of these two portraits cannot be denied, and in that vitality lies truth.

NOTES

1. In the case of this particular strip, forty-five newspapers, including the *Los Angeles Times*, even refused to run it (Nancy Sinatra 295).

2. The inclusion of *SNL* regular and Sinatra imitator Joe Piscopo's comments here underscore how much his imitations of Sinatra's singing are more of a loving tribute than authentic satire. Evidently uninterested in critiquing Sinatra or his music, Piscopo's approach was primarily comic: to juxtapose the rock music of everyone from Joan Jett, Foreigner, and Pat Benatar to Bruce Springsteen, Talking Heads, and the Rolling Stones with the more evident features of Sinatra's later, more mannerist, singing style. While hinting at the singer's being dated and suffering from Hollywood insincerity, his performances nonetheless reveal an intimate appreciation of Sinatra's recordings.

3. Trudeau tends to personalize his more generic metonymies. He pokes fun at Reagan's consciously perpetuated cowboy persona by drawing a western-style wooden fence, in disrepair, on the White House lawn in the foreground.

4. In fact, she uses two different versions of the song in *Nine Sinatra Songs*, although the choreographies for both share an optimistic view of love. The second is a live version from a Madison Square Garden concert when, according to Tharp, Sinatra's voice is "much more mature, his passion deeper, his commitment absolutely secure, as is the dancers'" (276).

PART I

SELF-PORTRAITS

CHAPTER 1

"Come [Fly, Dance, and Waltz] with Us on Equal Terms": The Whitmanesque Sinatra of Sammy Cahn

In his 1974 memoirs, *I Should Care*, lyricist Sammy Cahn (1913–1993) wrote: "I understand I'm considered to have 'put more words into Frank Sinatra's mouth than any other man' " (129). Given that it was Cahn, born Samuel Cohen, who penned the lyrics to such archetypal Sinatra hits as "Come Fly with Me," "All the Way," "My Kind of Town (Chicago Is)," "Three Coins in the Fountain," "All My Tomorrows," "Five Minutes More," "Ring-a-Ding-Ding," "Time after Time," and "The Tender Trap," to name but a very few, it is hard to argue with that premise. Of course, Cahn also said that he simply wrote songs and that it was the singer himself who made them "Sinatra songs." Such an assertion is, at best, only partially true. For coming from the mean streets of New York, Cahn shared with Sinatra many of the same formative experiences, influences, and attitudes, and that is why Frank himself said quite simply: "Sammy's words fit my mouth the best" (Lahr 62). But what helps to make Cahn's lyrical creations so appropriate, effective, and appealing is their blending of the quotidian and exceptional facets of Sinatra's persona. Like Walt Whitman's ideal "American Bard," Cahn's versions of "Sinatra" offer an exquisite combination of extravagance and humility, generosity and insatiability, immensity and accessibility.

The lexical and temperamental affinity Sinatra and Cahn shared, characterized by a fresh vernacular informality—what Cahn himself referred to as "meat-and-potatoes lyrics" (153)—can be keenly felt in many of the lyrics that Cahn wrote especially for the singer. During his autobiographical stage show, *Words and Music*, for example, Cahn used to joke about the repetitious chorus of "Five Minutes More," a number one song for Sinatra in 1946, in which he employed the title phrase four times within the space of sixteen bars. From a strictly compositional perspective, such repetition may seem a bit excessive, but when placed within their dramatic context, the lyrics, even with the "tin pan alley" rhymes, take on a very authentic feel. How many young men, when faced with the end of their evenings, which they had been anticipating all week long, are going to be able to muster a cogent and compelling argument? Driven by love, or something baser, the young man is far more likely to attempt to sway his lady with an earnestness revealed in the intense repetition of a simple and less-than-eloquent plea such as "five minutes more!" And, since Sinatra was well known for his focus on telling the story of a song, it should come as no surprise that the singer found such contextual integrity quite attractive and, most probably, quite familiar.

Sinatra, of course, greatly benefited from and rewarded the kinship he shared with the lyricist. It was, after all, Sammy Cahn whom Sinatra specifically requested that studio heads hire in 1945 as lyricist for his new musical film, *Anchors Aweigh*. "If you're not there on Monday, I'm not there Monday," the young star assured the songwriter (Cahn 134). They both were there on Monday, and Cahn would continue to write for him the rest of his life.[1] As a result, early on, it was Cahn's lyrics that helped Sinatra shape the naïve boy-next-door character that Sinatra would play in films like *Step Lively* (1944), *Anchors Aweigh*, *It Happened in Brooklyn* (1947), and *Double Dynamite* (1951), as well as other non-Cahn musicals like *The Kissing Bandit* (1948), *Take Me Out to the Ballgame* (1949), and *On the Town* (1949). With Cahn's help came the full flowering of the persona of the bow-tied young man about whom Bruce Bliven wrote in *The New Republic* in 1944: "He has a head of tousled black curls and holds it awkwardly to one side as he gestures clumsily and bashfully with his arms, trying to keep the crowd quiet enough for him to sing 'Embraceable You' " (Vare 22). Despite all the apparent awkwardness, however, Bliven knows that Sinatra performs "with sure showmanship and magnificent timing," well aware of how he must fulfill the image the bobby-soxers craved (Vare 22).

In the fifties, Cahn's lyrics, with their naturally informal diction, again "played a large part in building the image of the loosey-goosey, unpredictable ring-a-ding guy" (Lahr 64). The colloquialisms that expressed the nonchalant street swagger Cahn and Sinatra recognized in each other are also apparent in many of the lyricist's songs. For example, in the almost throwaway phrase, "kind of," in "Style," a celebration of sophistication and fashion written for Sinatra, Dean Martin, and Bing Crosby, from the 1964 film *Robin and the Seven Hoods*, the unpretentious identity of "Robbo" and his merry men is made manifest (emphasis added): "with mother-of-pearl *kind of* buttons, You'll look like the Astors and Huttons." Of course, Sinatra's keen fashion sense has been well documented,[2] and Cahn's task in writing (with Jimmy Van Heusen) the songs for this "Clan" film was to capture the individual personalities of the various members and highlight their unique talents in witty and winning ways.[3] At the same time, the lyrics, even such interjections as "kind of," were necessarily character-driven and needed to remain true to the *dramatis personae*.

Thus, more than simply a way of filling out the metrics of the line, the "kind of" betrays the regular fellows beneath the stylish clothes. They may dress like the wealthy, but underneath the designer clothes the two, and then three, of them are similar to all the guys who grew up streetwise like Cahn and Sinatra: a little rough around the edges but, due to their willingness to work hard, both well-deserving of the finer things in life and capable of developing a truly discriminating taste. As Walt Whitman, in his preface to the original 1855 edition of *Leaves of Grass*, writes of the democratic nature of the artist:

The American Bards . . . shall not be careful of riches and privilege . . . they shall be riches and privilege . . . [They] shall delineate no class of persons nor one or two out of the strata of interests nor love most nor truth most nor the soul most nor the body most . . . and not be for the eastern states more than the western or the northern states more than the southern. (14)

And Cahn's portrayal of Sinatra as an American everyman clearly resonated among the nation's males, as Pete Hamill forcefully argues in *Why Sinatra Matters*.[4]

Cahn's "Sinatra" is not, however, merely a man of the people; he is an iconic figure, as well. And the larger-than-life "Ring-a-Ding-Ding" image that the two built is not relegated merely to the more obvious

Sinatraesque songs as "Come Dance with Me," "Let Me Try Again," and what Cahn himself referred to as the quintessential Sinatra song, "I Like to Lead When I Dance." In fact, the image, too big to be contained, would permeate their collaborations from the 1950s onward.[5]

"Love and Marriage," written for the September 19, 1955, television musical version of Thornton Wilder's *Our Town*, for instance, would seem to be the epitome of a domesticated Sinatra. The familiar image of the horse and carriage recalls a simpler time, a more innocent age. Indeed, what the creators of the television series *Married with Children* were counting on when they chose it as their ironic theme song was that it embodied all the myths in which the fifties believed: a happily-ever-after life in the suburbs. Even the societal authorities the song cites attest to the apparently incontrovertible fact that love and marriage are a natural pair and, so the listener would think, a natural state. But what is to be made of *Sinatra's* singing this hymn to domesticity with an undeniably jaunty confidence?

On the one hand, he had every reason to be confident. By September 1955, Sinatra was, according to *Time* magazine, about to replace Bing Crosby as "the greatest all-around entertainer in show business" (Nancy Sinatra 122). He had won the Academy Award for *From Here to Eternity* in March of 1954, and his musical career was thriving once again with 1954's "top male vocalist" honors from *Billboard*, *Down Beat*, and *Metronome* magazines. On the other hand, it must be remembered that his own tumultuous second marriage to Ava Gardner finally had ended only the previous year, and everyone in America knew the turmoil and scandal that had consumed both of the stars. Frank had left his wife and children to be with Ava, after all. What could this guy know about love and marriage in a small town?

The central, but often overlooked, dynamic at play in "Love and Marriage," which would reach number five during seventeen weeks on the single charts and become the first song to win an Emmy Award, is the fact that Sinatra sang it as the "Stage Manager" in *Our Town*. The play, of course, centers upon "a typical New England American town— its people, their births, lives, deaths, and meaning in the scheme of things" (Cahn 153). As the stage manager, however, Sinatra differs significantly from the other characters in the play; he stands separate from the people who live in Grover's Corners.

Sinatra's relationship with this mid-1950s audience can be seen to have been quite similar. The audience knew that he, as the singer who most effectively chronicled their loves and losses, was connected intimately to them, but, at the same time, they had to have appreciated that the same rules did not, maybe even could not, apply to him. And Cahn recognized how well the role fit Sinatra, because, according to the lyricist: "ever since I've known him Sinatra likes to stroll on and stroll off, just like that stage manager does throughout the play, telling the audience what's what"(154). This is precisely what he does in the song: he tells his audience about these *other* characters' lives, about the truths that govern *their* lives. Consequently, when Sinatra sings that love and marriage are inseparable, the listening audience cannot help but sense that, while they cannot sever them, *he* most probably can. The song undeniably celebrates marriage and domesticity, but the singer's performance of it, accompanied by the frisky Nelson Riddle arrangement, makes it very clear that he means it for somebody else. The beauty of so many of Cahn's songs for Sinatra, therefore, is that, through them, everybody can share in that freedom from convention that the singer embodies. A figure who is simultaneously and believably "one of the guys" *and* peerless, that is the remarkably Whitmanesque creation of Sammy Cahn's "Sinatra."[6]

In the early 1960s, as Frank Sinatra became a force with which to be reckoned in the capitals of both the entertainment world and, due to his connection to Kennedy's "Camelot," American politics, so Cahn's exceptional "Sinatra" would begin to loom larger and larger on the cultural landscape, as well. Nowhere is this better illustrated than in the Cahn and Van Heusen composition "California."

"California" was recorded by Sinatra on February 20, 1963, during his sessions for the album *The Concert Sinatra*. Arranged and conducted by Nelson Riddle, the song, a paean to the "Golden State," celebrates the natural grandeur and beauty that is California. Performed in the grand, orchestral style of other songs from *The Concert Sinatra* sessions, such as "You'll Never Walk Alone," "Ol' Man River," and "Lost in the Stars," and paired on a promotional recording of "America the Beautiful," "California" begs to be understood in a solidly patriotic and straightforward manner. In fact, Will Friedwald in *The Song Is You* expresses surprise and regret that Sinatra did not include it on his "deadly serious" album of 1964 with Bing Crosby and Fred Waring, which was "apparently inspired, like Judy Garland's 'Battle Hymn of the Republic,' by the murder of the President" (Friedwald 417). The problem is that the text of the song argues against such a simple interpretation. Here are the lyrics in full:

I've known her valleys.
I've known her mountains,

her missions, and her courtyards, and her fountains,
the giant redwoods towering in the skies of her
that grow as though they know they show the size of her.   5
I've often wandered her farthest reaches,
her desert sands, her snows, and, yes, her beaches.
A land that paradise could well be jealous of
That's California, California,
blessed by heaven from above.   10
That's California, the land I love.[7]

While undoubtedly stunning in its arrangement, on the structural level
a seriously patriotic reading is prevented (or, at the very least, severely
hindered) by the comic rhyming in the fifth line. Owing far more to the
wordplay of an Irving Berlin or Ira Gershwin than the sober "spacious
skies" and "pilgrim feet" of "America the Beautiful," Cahn's linking of
"grow," "though," "know," and "show," in a single line—even as the
long vowels suggest the Golden State's richness and opulence—reveals
the waggish sensibility of a man who holds the world on a string.[8]

More significantly, Cahn's lyrics wittily betray a familiar Sinatra spirit
through the employment of the archaic sexual definition of the verb "to
know." The singer's "knowledge" of the state is clearly carnal and further emphasized by both Cahn's use of the feminine possessive pronoun "her" and the *double entendre* inherent in "valleys" and "mountains." The depiction of the state in openly erotic terms, thus, taps into
and fosters the very image and lifestyle Sinatra and Cahn in the Rat Pack
era were publicly fostering.[9]

Of course, rendering the American landscape as a woman was nothing new. Much has been written about what Annette Kolodny refers to
as the "psychosexual dynamic of a virginal paradise" in which the earliest writers on the "New World" consistently engaged by eroticizing
the American wilderness. Indeed, the practice was so thorough that
the use of sexual metaphors for discovery and settlement came to con-
stitute "a cognitive component in the writing of history" (Kolodny 3).
In "California," then, as America herself had been since the Europeans
dropped anchor, the "Eureka State" was here for the taking, in every
sense of the word.

More meaningfully, however, the erotic dimension of the song's image posits Sinatra, for whom the song was written, not simply as a man
with a prodigious sexual past—how many of us have had the chance to
know even a "Poor Little Rhode Island,"[10] much less California?—but
also as the ultimate American artist, who must: "attract his own land
body and soul to himself and hang on its neck with incomparable love

and plunge his semitic muscle into its merits and demerits" (Whitman 21). Intimately familiar with his world, Whitman's poet/artist/creator cannot sit back and contemplate; he must act lavishly and procreatively. And who better than Cahn's "Sinatra" fits Whitman's description: "The known universe has one complete lover and that is the greatest poet . . . His love above all love has leisure and expanse . . . he leaves room ahead of himself. He is no irresolute or suspicious lover . . . he is sure . . . he scorns intervals. (11). In "California," Sinatra fully becomes such a Whitmanesque lover: patriotic, grand, generous, and unbounded.[11]

Not coincidentally, this understanding of "California" as a song of sexual conquest also completes the metamorphosis of Sinatra's image from the sexually inexperienced boy of the 1940s into the man literally on top of the world during the 1950s and early 1960s. One of the first Cahn lyrics that the singer performed in 1944's *Step Lively* also made use of an exploration and discovery theme, but "Come Out, Come Out, Wherever You Are," with music by Jule Styne, only highlights the differences between the singer and the explorers:

> Columbus had more chance than me
> When he set sail to cross the sea.
> At least he thought he knew what he was doing.
> I'm in search of something too,
> Exactly what I wish I knew.
> Yes, I pursue, but who am I pursuing?
> Chances are that I won't find a bride,
> But it won't be because I haven't tried.

Clueless in his quest, the young singer can only hope to stumble upon a prize. In "California," Cahn returns to this image of Sinatra as conquistador. In 1963, however, the well-traveled singer, who had helped to show his fans the way, had become himself an intimate and formidable part of the American landscape.

In Cahn's lyrics, therefore, Sinatra comes to embody both the egalitarian and semidivine dimensions with which Whitman infused his conception of the ultimate American artist. Recognizably humble in origins and consequently approachable, but also operating on a plane unreachable by most people, the artist summons all to partake of his abundance. As Whitman suggests: "The messages of the great poets to each man and woman are, Come to us on equal terms, Only then can you understand us, We are no better than you, What we enclose you enclose, What we enjoy you may enjoy" (13). In the same way, Frank's performance of Cahn's lyrical invitations to "come fly," "come dance," and "come waltz" with him warmly bids his listeners to partake of his artistic largess, to live the way he lives—even if only vicariously through song.

NOTES

1. When the lifelong Democrat Sinatra started palling around with Republicans, Cahn continued to supply him with "special lyrics"— even for rallies for Vice President Spiro Agnew. As the lyricist unapologetically told the appalled Kennedys: "I'll always write for Frank whenever he asks me" (Cahn 146).

2. See Bill Zehme's 1997 *The Way You Wear Your Hat.*

3. Cahn and Van Heusen (1913–1990), for example, wrote the song and dance number "Bang Bang" for Sammy Davis, Jr.; the sentimental ballad "Any Man Who Loves His Mother" for Dean Martin; and—parodying his saintly *Going My Way* persona—"Don't Be a Do-Badder" for Bing Crosby.

4. The colloquial nature of Cahn's lyrics also recalls the nineteenth-century poet's love of the integrity of American English. As Whitman writes with a typical disregard for grammar: "It is the chosen tongue to express growth faith self-esteem freedom justice equality friendliness amplitude prudence decision and courage." (23)

5. In fact, by the time Sinatra would record Cahn's "Love Makes Us Whatever We Want to Be" in 1982, the lyrics would so empower Sinatra that he could tell the listener to ignore the musical accompaniment altogether.

6. Compare the comment made by the fictional Finkie Finklestein in the 1999 epistolary novel *Sinatraland* (discussed in chapter 11), in which he confesses to Frank his and every other man's insecurity . . . every man, that is, except Frank (Kashner 76).

7. Since many of the details specifically mentioned in Cahn's lyrics also appear in the unofficial state song of the time, "I Love You, California," it seems clear that Cahn was at least vaguely familiar with it. The F.B. Silverwood/Alfred Frankenstein composition, while only legally ratified as the state song in 1988, had been around since the 1915 San Francisco and San Diego expositions and had been, unofficially, the state song since 1951. Cahn's significant contribution was to turn a chastely patriotic profession of love into a flag-waving song of sexual conquest and, as a result, to place the state and the singer on a mythic scale.

8. The colloquial interjection of "yes" also undercuts a purely reverential reading of the song (Cahn's "California," l. 7).

9. The single was "only sent to radio stations, and the recordings were never commercially released" until the four-CD boxed set, *The Reprise Collection* (Marino and Furfeo 204).

10. "Poor Little Rhode Island" is the title of a song that Cahn had cowritten with Jule Styne in 1944.

11. One might argue that perhaps Friedwald is correct in thinking it was a mistake for Sinatra to omit the song from 1964's *America, I Hear You Singing* with Crosby and Waring (Friedwald's *The Song Is You* 417). Given Sinatra's storied past with John "Chickee Boy" Kennedy and women like Judith Campbell Exner, the blatantly sexual aspect might have made it a perversely appropriate tribute.

CHAPTER 2

The Colors of Ava: *Tone Poems of Color* and the Painful Measure of Sinatra's Passions

While it may seem odd in a book about the imagery of Sinatra to dedicate an entire chapter to a mostly unfamiliar 1956 album on which he does not even sing, *Tone Poems of Color* was not just another Sinatra album. For, although millions around the world recognize Sinatra as a singer, movie actor, and television personality, not to mention a generous philanthropist and consistent fodder for the tabloids, few know about his love of conducting. Throughout his career, however, at the points when he most possessed the clout to do things his way, he seemed to turn to conducting, at least briefly. This must say something about the image he had of himself.

In 1945, for example, at the height of "Sinatrauma," the young singer surprised everyone when he convinced Columbia Records executives to allow him, an untrained pop star adored by millions of teen-aged girls, to conduct an album of Alec Wilder's "classical" compositions. At Capitol Records, after his resurgence as one of the most powerful forces in Hollywood, he again would take up the baton for albums by Peggy Lee (*The Man I Love*, 1957) and Dean Martin (*Sleep Warm*, 1958). And after he began his own record company, Reprise, in 1960—

and once he had recorded enough songs for seven vocal albums to compete in sales with his brilliant Capitol catalogue—he recorded *Frank Sinatra Conducts Music from Pictures and Plays* in June 1962. He would conduct yet again, following his critically acclaimed return to recording in the early 1980s, on albums for longtime friend, cabaret singer Sylvia Syms (*Syms by Sinatra*, 1982), and trumpeter Charles Turner (*What's New*, 1983). Indeed, on *The Future*, the third record of 1979's *Trilogy: The Past, Present, and Future*, Sinatra, through the libretto of Gordon Jenkins, waxes eloquent on his love of conducting:

> Given a choice, I would choose
> To have a magic wand that I could use
> To draw a melody from the enchanted maze of brass
> And keys and wood and wind and steel.
> And I would stand there, big and brave, and quietly say
> "Ladies and Gentlemen . . . Play for me . . . Play for me."

"This was brave," indeed, for record buyers never really had shown interest in Sinatra the conductor, but, then again, Sinatra rarely gave the public exactly what they expected.

And so, back in February and March 1956, it should have come as no surprise that, as Capitol's premier star, he would inaugurate its brand new recording studios, the now familiar "stack of records" building, with a session of his own choosing. Sinatra was, after all, the singer who, since arriving at Capitol in April 1953, had returned nearly to the top of the album charts with three separate LPs (*Songs for Young Lovers*, *Swing Easy*, and *In the Wee Small Hours*) and the singles top ten charts four times ("Young at Heart," "Three Coins in the Fountain," "Learning the Blues," and "Love and Marriage"). As an actor, he had won an Academy Award for Best Supporting Actor in *From Here to Eternity* in 1954, and recently had starred in several films, both dramatic (*Suddenly*, *Not as a Stranger*, and Otto Preminger's *The Man with the Golden Arm*)[1] and musical (*Guys and Dolls*, *The Tender Trap*).[2] On television, in September 1955, he would star in an Emmy-winning musical version of Thornton Wilder's *Our Town*. Sinatra, in short, was at the very height of his powers and popularity.

Given his commercial and artistic success in so many media, Sinatra's choice of *Tone Poems of Color* to inaugurate the new Capitol studios is a fascinating one. The ambitious project, for which Sinatra, as both producer and conductor, solicited musical settings by composers Nelson Riddle, Billy May, Gordon Jenkins, Victor Young, Alec Wilder, Jeff Alexander, Andre Previn, and Elmer Bernstein, was based on a series of poems by Norman Sickel, described in the album's liner notes only as a "writer of past Sinatra radio shows." What is so intriguing about the album, however, is that everything about the project-from its instrumental nature and song sequencing to its remarkably dark and unromantic manner—defies expectations. The title, *Tone Poems of Color*, if it elicits any reaction at all, perhaps evokes innocuous mental pictures of rainbows or kaleidoscopes. This is hardly the case; both the individual poems and their ordering haunt the reader with their darkness. By shunning sentimentalism at every turn, the poems avoid the easily affirming and, through an emotional richness, depict a tortured universe in which greed, haughtiness, violence, and intrigue overpower laughter, love, and innocence. And it was this sense of the uncertainty inherent in, and depicted by, the extraordinary project to which Sinatra was drawn.

In the sequence of twelve free-verse poems, ranging in length from twenty-four to thirty-two staccato lines, Norman Sickel conceived a specific character for each of the colors. Green, for example, is the "lover," yellow "laughter," orange the "gay deceiver," silver "the patrician," etc. The poems, however, are not discrete units. The poet carefully parallels the colors by highlighting both their close kinship and distinct contrasts to each other. Pairs such as gold and yellow, silver and gray, or purple and orange, for instance, are connected directly but clearly differentiated. Gold "only *reflects* the warmth of Mother yellow" (4–5), and silver had been gray "til [it] was shined to meet / the people" (5–6). And it is these interrelationships between the color/ characters that allow the album to develop a narrative tension. The poems achieve this tension by consistently foreshadowing and recalling each other while highlighting, in a very real way, the true consanguinity of the colors—that is, the very subtle distinctions between radically different emotions all along the psychological spectrum.

Often Sickel's subtleties prove perceptive. For example, both orange, the "gay deceiver," and purple, the political, self-destructive "schemer," share the violent red. But, whereas orange softens the threat of red with the sunny laughter of yellow, the red in purple brings out blue's more ominously deceitful quality. The results are telling: In "Orange," for example, the sunny yellow situates the deception of orange within a romantic context—but without changing the essentially dangerous quality of the red. The context suggests flirtation or seduction, but the language conveys a physicality that approaches sexual assault (emphasis added):

[I] smile a smile
as does yellow,
but a studied smile
pushed through painted
   red lips
into minds of men
who receive, enjoy . . .
but not really enjoy. (18–25)

In "Purple," meanwhile, the seductive peril is heightened even more, in both its intensity and societal context by blue's dreams of power. What had been sexual conquest in "Orange" turns to a royal power struggle:

My padded footsteps roam
   the earth
but only by night;
its dark blue dreamy shroud
cloaking my violent red
   thoughts. (4–9)

By poem's end, purple's own "regal-shaded velvet glove" (22–23) is "choking [itself] with intrigue" (20). Thus, for all the big dreams of blue, the schemes for political domination have suffocated him and left him as empty and alone as the shallow orange deceiver.

Nor do the colors always blend the same way. In "Purple," blue "cloaks" the red. In "Green," however, "blue is "wedded" (26) to yellow, and, as a result, "love only grows" (5):

My blue dreams smile
for laughing yellow is
   there too
and smiles into our
dreams. (10–14)

Thus, instead of a suicidal and ill-fated lust for power, a "living, loving reality" (19–20) grows even stronger. It is all in the mix.

Despite the inventiveness and subtle execution of Sickel's controlling conceit, the poems themselves will never be confused with Wordsworth. While avoiding the cliched green of jealousy and the gray of old age, Sickel's poetry still tends to use rather traditional imagery (e.g., gold representing greed, purple royalty, and brown Mother Earth). And the poet does turn an infelicitous phrase at times, as in "Yellow," when the sun-worshipping child reaches for the:

life-giving
purifying rays of the
world's heating system. (12–14)

Despite such occasional failings, it is not difficult to see the dramatic possibilities Sinatra perceived in the interrelation of the colors, and exploit them Sinatra does. For the arc of the album is surprisingly dramatic and quite contrary to what one would expect.

The order of the colors does not correspond directly to any simple or recognizable pattern (white, green, purple, yellow, gray, and gold on Side One, with orange, black, silver, blue, brown, and red on Side Two), and, consequently, the order demands attention. For example, the album starts with the innocence and liveliness of "White" and "Green," while utilizing marital imagery to introduce both the blamelessness of the former and the mixed, but vital, nature of the latter. White is "the young in heart" (1–2),[3] and green the union of laughing yellow and dreaming blue. Of course, marriage is a traditionally comic *ending* in literature that suggests the reaffirmation of society. In *Tone Poems*, marriage initiates the piece on an upbeat note, but it would seem to leave open only a path toward disintegration and isolation, which is exactly what occurs. The album ends hauntingly with the jealous violence of "Red's" cutting the beautiful white skin of a rival.[4] Far from reassuring, the sequence only disturbs. And, again and again, the order of the colors defies such expectations.

The expectations of the listener/reader regarding the remainder of the album, after the first four selections, are decidedly auspicious. Three of the first four are positive in language, imagery, and tone. Only in the mixing of the dreamy blue with violent red to make purple does the vivid image of self-destruction upset a blessed world of innocence (white),[5] love (green), and laughter (yellow). Beginning with "Gray," however, the world turns much more discouraging.

"Gaunt" gray seeks "to fill the love-starved hollows of his cheeks and heart" (3–6). Gold is "metallic and unyielding" (8–9) and knows that it can possess "everything but happiness" (25–26). Superficial orange is "correct / and stylish" (12–13), but its shade "will never . . . pierce [its] skin / to affect [its] soul" (14–16). Silver only wants to be left "alone / to live [its] life / in a velvet lined drawer" (19–21), while "Red" is an all-consuming violence. In fact, of the final eight selections, only "Black," "Blue," and "Brown" offer anything remotely positive, and in the cases of the first two, the positives are considerably qualified.

The dreamer in "Blue," for example, while indeed blue, is not sad. Nevertheless, the dreams of this blue-eyed man[6] who is yet a "boy-at-heart" (13) only result in happiness by "cloud[ing] reality" (15–16). One must ask what kind of happiness this is, how authentic it could be, if it obscures truth. And the answer to this question is especially problematic when one recalls that in "Green" (on Side One) the eyes of youth, in all their warmth and holiness, are "unclouded" (20), and in "Yellow" love is a "living . . . reality" (19–20). Nor can it be forgotten that "Blue" shares in the creation of the scheming and suicidal "Purple."

"Black," the color that probably possesses the longest tradition of negative connotations in Western literature, is given a slightly favorable twist here. The color, although still embodying "the bottomless / the fog I cannot lift" (1–2), is not unconquerable. In fact, it is the bottomless nature of black that allows "thoughts of deeds" finally to "bring reflection and rest" (14–15). Just as in "Blue," in which the dreamer has "made a friend of sadness" (4–5), here, by the conclusion of the poem:

> Black
> is my friend
> though it be bottomless. (26–28)

Only "Brown," which is "Mother Nature," offers a union, a marriage, as it were, of the aforementioned colors. And it is this penultimate poem of the album that would have been a natural, and orderly, conclusion for the album, for as "Mother Earth":

> I change my dress
> as seasons change
> but ever do return
> to brown. (8–11)

Implied in this seasonal image is the transformation of colors, including the green and yellow of spring and summer, as well as the red and orange of autumn. Yet, even as the leaves turn multicolored, so they all eventually "change their / shade / to match my face" (16–18). Thus, like gray (not coincidentally the penultimate song of Side One), brown comprises the other colors within it. Unlike gray, however, brown does not "rob the spectrum of all colors" (8–10) and turn everything "monotone" (25). Rather, through the very cycle of nature herself, brown shares more in the vitality of green and the "life-giving rays" (12–13) of yellow than in the "square" futility of gray (26).

By concluding the album with "Brown," therefore, all the previous colors would have been tied together into a natural unit and would have become part of the natural course of the universe. The ugliness of the scheming purple, the aloof silver, or superficial orange—instead of representing the worst of society—would have been subsumed by Mother Earth in what could be seen as a conciliatory and reaffirming gesture of unity. Such a gesture is not offered here, however. Instead, the listener is offered one more color, the violent red.

"Red," as seen above, had been introduced previously in both "Purple" and "Orange," harshly altering the character of the dreamy "Blue" and radiant "Yellow." Here, however, it shows itself in all of its unadulterated and consuming violence:

> streak[ing] for the
>   whiteness of her skin
> until nothing satisfied [her]
> nothing
> only the brightly hot
>   lines of red
> glowing on her skin (22–28)

The imagery of the red lines on the white flesh sardonically recalls the very first song, "White," in the spotless innocence of the cradle and wedding. By the end, however, the pure white of marriage is stained with the violent attack of jealousy, and what had been a loving union in "White" is now seen in the objectifying terms of "possession" in "Red" (19).

Of course, this sexual violence does not come, as it were, out of the blue; it had been foreshadowed at least since the beginning of Side Two in the emblematic sexual assault by "Orange" discussed above. In "Orange," however, the more figurative attack was perpetrated by a woman as she speaks of seducing a man; here the woman physically attacks another woman over the possession of a man, raising questions about the gender issues of the poetry.

Throughout Sinatra's musical career, his collaborators were rarely women. Of course, on record, film, radio, and television, he performed with a wide variety of women: from Dinah Shore, Ella Fitzgerald, Rosemary Clooney, and Judy Garland to Keely Smith, Pearl Bailey, daughter Nancy, and Dagmar. Nevertheless, the vast majority of the arrangers, conductors, and musicians were male, and the personnel of the *Tone Poems* project were no different: Sinatra, Sickel, Riddle, Jenkins, May, Alexander, Wilder, Young, Previn, and Bernstein. Given the era (the

mid-1950s), this male dominance is hardly surprising, and in the case of
Tone Poems of Color, the very gendered nature of the texts reveals itself
repeatedly.

Of the twelve poems, five of the six colors that are clearly gender-spe-
cific are rendered as females: white, yellow, orange, brown, and red.
Only "Blue" specifically mentions that "I am a man" (11). One other,
"Black," by embodying the void, eschews personification altogether.
Given the long tradition of men's feminizing everything from the
moon and liberty to ships and cars, this ratio of the specifically female to
specifically male is not surprising.

Also not surprising is the sense that, despite the heavily feminine nature of the personification, Sickel's "default setting" for gender is mas-
culine. Although the remaining five depictions are ambiguous (i.e.,
while personified, they display no clear identification of gender such as
a pronoun or other such specific designation), certain images and language clearly suggest a male voice in three of them. "Gold," for example, is described only as the "child of Mother Yellow" (5–6), but the
elaborate mining conceit infers a son. Similarly, the detached patrician
in "Silver," despite speaking in terms of an "orderly" house that
"gleams" (7–8) and carpets which "bear no / footprints" (9–10), implies more an anal-retentive male than a fussy, homemaking wife. The
cleanliness of the house emphasizes the sterile distance he wishes to
maintain from the common mob rather than the pride of one who over-
sees, much less does, the actual labor. The Latin root of "patrician" suggests a male hierarchy, as well. The brutal suffocation capping the
palace intrigue in "Purple" also strongly indicates a male, though, admittedly, not in as conclusive a fashion.

The "love-starved" (4) gray, who "robs the spectrum" (8–9), embodies the most omnivorous and least satisfied of the colors. After all, it
receives no solace from the laughter of female yellow, the dreams of
male blue, or even the love of indeterminate green (11–16). And, as if
to heighten the sense of wanting, even the poem's imagery refuses to
contain itself to a single conceit, painting, or music:

> I take them all to my
> bosom
> to make into one;
> one for me alone.
> And yet
> when my brush is done,
> it is only monotone;
> a square and futile fugue

and I am left alone
without a rounded life. (17–26)

Music/painting, male/female, gray blur the divisions until all are re-
duced to the same hue. The result, however, is not bisexual or her-
maphroditic as much as nondescript, empty, and asexual.

The color most ambiguous in gender is, without a doubt, the lover in
"Green":

I walk through the years
but never alone
for I am loved,
and on my path beside me
is my love. (21–25)

By whom is this spoken, a man or a woman? Earlier in the poem, when
Sickel focuses on the lavish growth of the love they share, the imagery is
even less definitive, being more horticultural than romantic:

As I love
I plant a seed
and my thumb is green,
and makes it grow
into a living, loving
    reality. (15–20)

Despite (or because of) the imprecision, Sickel's meaning seems obvious: love is the same whether the lover is male or female; love is a natural
force that transcends gender considerations and even human institu-
tions; as Vergil wrote in *Eclogue* 10, *omnia vincit amor*, "love conquers
all." But, it must be asked, if love is so powerful, why does "Green," only
the second poem, come so early in the sequence? Why must omnipotent
love be so utterly forgotten by the time red leaves her bloody scratches
on the white skin of her rival? The logic of the sequence here is not so apparent, and Mother Nature's embrace of the color spectrum, offered in
the album's penultimate "Brown," seems even less placating now.

And it is in the less-than-comforting conclusion of the cycle that its
character finally and fully is revealed. Concluding with the images of a
pair of powerfully threatening, albeit traditionally characterized
women, *Tone Poems of Color* conveys something quite elemental about
the mid-50s Sinatra: his attraction, since his comeback, of more male
than female fans. As Pete Hamill writes, Sinatra started attracting more
male fans because: "[Men] identified with the personal drama of the

Fall, with the cliché of the hero led astray by the vixen and his eventual release from her wiles. Or they embraced another cliché: he had paid his dues" (176). Sinatra had won over all those men by showing that, unlike the boy with the ethereal voice who had made the bobby-soxers swoon, now older and wiser, he could sing with the "voice of a man" (Hamill 177). This wisdom came of heartbreak and loss, of defeat and—what mattered most to this new audience—survival: "There was rue in some of the songs. There was regret, There was no self-pity." (Hamill 177). His remarkable return to success was evidence that one could more than survive defeat, that one could succeed even more the second time around.

And that survival, in a sense, is what Sinatra's classic 1955 LP *In the Wee Small Hours* celebrates. The heartache that so characterized the tale of his love of Ava Gardner not only did not destroy him (though it seemed to come very close), it helped make him capable of producing a true work of art. The sheer beauty of "the Voice" of the 1940s was gone, but in its place was an artist accomplished enough to bring to his singing an emotional intensity and honesty uncommon in popular music. And yet, even as he sings of utter loss on *In the Wee Small Hours*, his performance implies that loss is not the end. In fact, it proves that, with each listening, such a cathartic experience can allow the audience (as it had allowed Sinatra himself) to climb out of the ruins and begin anew. For example, the final song of *In the Wee Small Hours* is "This Love of Mine," a song Sinatra originally recorded with Tommy Dorsey in 1941 and for which he received cowriting credit. By revisiting the song in 1955, the singer both offers a more mature and realistic understanding of a love that goes on and on and ameliorates the sense of despair treated by the album. It offers hope even in the face of heartbreak.

On *Tone Poems*, however, with the early departure of the green lovers and yellow laughter, the combination of a cathartic release and a sense of hope is more difficult to support. Here, the female figures that dominate the second half of the cycle, especially the vixen Red (to paraphrase Hamill), make Sinatra's release from Ava's wiles seem far less certain. In short, the vulnerability that Sinatra undoubtedly reveals on *In the Wee Small Hours* is considerably multiplied here.

Philip Furia has argued persuasively for how the dramatic power of many of Sinatra's standards derives from their being written for Broadway musicals and, more often than not, for the women in these shows. The necessary changes in the lyrics, to have them make sense when sung by a man, tend to emphasize a vulnerability that songs written exclusively for the swinging Sinatra ("Come Fly with Me," for example) lack. As Furia writes, Sinatra's adaptation of these lyrics allowed him: "to project, beyond his street-wise, tough-guy stage presence, a poignant, vulnerable, and 'lost' persona" (165). By recording these "women's songs," Sinatra could plumb the depths of his own emotional despair and, consequently, through the songs' beauty link the power of love to the danger of leaving oneself unguarded and exposed.

The conclusion of *Tone Poems of Color* with its pair of strong women, earth mother and whore, also reflects a vulnerability, but, in contrast, here it is one apparently born more of fear than sensitivity. The sequence shows a conductor/producer who, as he wields his phallic baton,[7] seems less interested in unearthing the fragility of love than in exerting a control over the women who populate the sequence, perhaps an attractive alternative at this point in his career and life. The patriarchal nature of classical music has long been recognized, and Sinatra's employment of it, especially as a show of both professional clout and musical legitimacy, quite natural. As the opportunity to officially produce an album for the first time (Friedwald, *The Song Is You* 366), the *Tone Poems* project would bear his stamp completely, and this sense of control seems to be, in many ways, with what the album is ultimately concerned.

Nevertheless, what the interrelationships and sequencing of the pieces suggest most of all is a feeling of impotence, or, at the very least, of defensiveness. Despite being aimed at a male audience and utilizing familiar (and hence controllable) images of women, the text of *Tone Poems of Color* undermines the confidence Sinatra attempts to exude in the music. Instead of reveling in the command afforded him as conductor and producer, his choice of the poems and their arrangement betrays the ugliness and wariness at the root of his project.

On the eve of their breakup, Ava Gardner was quoted as saying: "When [Frank] was down and out he was sweet. Now that he's got successful again, he's become his old arrogant self. We were happy when he was on the skids" (Holder 96). There is a recognizable arrogance in *Tone Poems*, and it is one that barely conceals the bitterness of Ava's painful legacy, his sense of her having left him bloodied and alone. On *In the Wee Small Hours*, Sinatra could capture the exquisite communion of love and loss, and on its follow-up, *Songs for Swingin' Lovers*, he could celebrate the feeling of being free to enjoy women again now that he was released from their clutches. In *Tone Poems of Color*, however, the experience depicted is much more disagreeable for, with love sent packing so early, the only thing left at the end is the distrust and the ache.

NOTES

1. He would receive a "Best Actor" nomination for *The Man with the Golden Arm*.

2. Only a month before *Tone Poems*, Sinatra had finished recording the songs for his next film project, Cole Porter's *High Society*, with Bing Crosby, Grace Kelly, Celeste Holm, and Louis Armstrong.

3. The allusion to Sinatra's hit song, "Young at Heart," which lasted twenty-two weeks on *Billboard*'s Singles Chart beginning in February 1954, should not be dismissed too quickly. It very clearly, but subtly, links the conducting Sinatra with the more popular singer without blatantly (i.e., musically) recalling the singer's more familiar vocal performances.

4. One might be tempted to argue that, in 1956, perhaps "Red" with its cold war/communist implications was where the cycle had to end, but the poet's treatment of the color more as a fallen woman than a political threat would seem to refute such a reading.

5. It should be noted that even the innocence of "White" is not entirely pure. "Mother tears" still must "wash away /the grimes of deeds / she did not mean to do" (16-20). Nevertheless, the possibility (and probability) of the forgiveness of these sins is central to the opening poem. Even having committed these acts, white opens the album having been redeemed. This religious dimension is reiterated in the forgiveness of the "purifying rays" (13) of "Yellow," the fourth song, in which the son "seeks nothing . . . but his direct / happy-filled / communication / from his Holy Father" (21-25).

6. Little, if anything, should be made of the blue eyes here. Sinatra would not become known as "ol' Blue Eyes" until after his return from retirement in the early seventies. Mention of Sinatra's eye color in the press prior to 1973 is rare. One also would be committing serious anachronism (while making Sickel eerily prescient) to see anything in the following from "Purple" (emphasis added):

> I plan red plans to move
>   mountains
> *my way.* (11–13)

7. One cannot help but wonder if Sinatra was being playfully Freudian in his insertion of "small" in the latter part of his March 1948 recording of Irving Berlin's sweetly phallic "Fella with an Umbrella."

CHAPTER 3

The Composition of Celebrity: Sinatra as Text in the Liner Notes of Stan Cornyn

In late 1995, when Reprise Records released its limited edition twenty-CD boxed set, *Frank Sinatra: The Complete Reprise Studio Recordings*, it was decidedly appropriate that the producers devoted approximately a quarter of the ninety-six-page hardcover book included in the set to "Eye Witness," an essay by Stan Cornyn. Since 1964, Cornyn has been, in a very tangible—if somewhat paradoxical—way, the voice of Frank Sinatra. For it is his distinctive voice in the liner notes[1] that sets the stage and mood of sixteen Sinatra albums[2] . . . even before the first note is heard, the first lyric sung.[3] Pregnant with dramatic images, hepcat language, and tortured syntax, Cornyn's lyricism would be elemental in both capturing and promulgating the Sinatra image at the very peak of his celebrity: entertainer and artist, cynic and romantic, survivor and star.

Twice winner of the Grammy Award for "Album Notes (Annotator's Award)" and nominated five times in all (Kaplan 325, 329, 334, 336, 354), Cornyn celebrates Sinatra's preeminent status as "The Chairman of the Board"[4] by wrapping him in images and cadences so distinctive and individual that they become integral to Sinatra's albums and almost inseparable from the recordings themselves.[5] Cornyn's annotation for the 1967 LP *Frank Sinatra: The World We Knew* is found, after all, on the FRONT cover and, by 1969, Cornyn only needed to initial his *My Way* notes.[6] In the end, Cornyn's mix of "New Journalistic" detail and bardic intonation would play a major role in the creation of the iconic Sinatra: the man who lives our life, the artist who gives us voice.

Cornyn's annotation of Sinatra albums began rather modestly on *It Might As Well Be Swing* (1964), the second collaboration between Sinatra and Count Basie, with a back cover interview of the album's arranger/conductor, Quincy Jones. Such interviews would comprise three of the first five liner notes Cornyn would write for the artist. The "conversation" with Jones, as would the subsequent interviews of producers Jimmy Bowen and Sonny Burke for *Sinatra 65* (1965) and *My Kind of Broadway* (1965), respectively, covers a variety of topics but focuses primarily upon the process of preparing and recording the albums: song selection, chart writing, and, most significantly, the working relationship of the musicians, conductors, and singer during the sessions themselves. What becomes clear in all three interviews is that Sinatra is not merely a great popular singer but a great musician as well:

Jones: And Basie's drummer, Sonny Payne, remarked at the time what a pleasure it was to work with so musical a singer and to work, moreover with a man who, in a sense, was able to swing him.

Bowen: [The musicians] are honored to be there. Hal Blaine, my drummer, fourteen years he waited to play on a Frank Sinatra session. I never forget [*sic*] when I first called him on the phone and I said "Frank Sinatra date" he didn't say nothing for three minutes. I think he fainted.

Burke: The guys he works with are pros, and he's a pro's pro.

Cornyn's focus on the artistic process of Sinatra's recording would predominate even more on *Softly As I Leave You* (1964). But instead of simply reporting the reflections of participants in the recording session, Cornyn takes his readers there:

He walks into a recording session about a half an hour after the orchestra has begun running down the songs. He looks smart, what your mother used to call "natty." His wide-banded hat is tipped back, one inch off straight flat. He doesn't come in with a fanfare. He's there though. He strolls through the studio obstacle course, the mike booms, the cable spaghetti, the music stands. Softly and with a grin he greets the musicians who've been working his sessions for years. "Hi ye, Sweets." "Evenin' sunshine."

Here the annotator clearly has begun to co-opt the methods and techniques of the "New Journalism" which newspaper and magazine writers such as Gay Talese, Jimmy Breslin, and Tom Wolfe were only beginning to develop in the early sixties (Wolfe 34–37).[7]

The "New Journalism" essentially applied the techniques of fiction writing to reporting. First and foremost, according to Wolfe in his seminal 1972 *New York Magazine* essay, the new approach demanded a level of detail only to be gleaned by the reporter's "arriving on the scene before the main event in order to gather the off-camera material, the by-play in the make-up room, that would enable him to create character" (38). These details, however, were communicated through the strategies traditionally associated with the novelist: the distinctive narrative voice of "someone who was actually on the scene and involved in it" (Wolfe 38), chameleon-like switches in points of view (43), and the "lavish" use of any number of more literary "mannerisms," such as interjection, pleonasm, and the historical present (45). As Wolfe writes: "The idea was to give the full objective description plus something that readers had always had to go to novels and short stories for: the subjective or emotional life of the characters" (45).

In his *Softly As I Leave You* liner notes, Cornyn for the first time takes his readers to the recording session to see, hear, and, to some extent, be the artist at work. Cornyn also begins to develop a basic paradigm of anticipation, entrance, performance, and appreciation[8] by which he attempts to capture everyone present in the studio, a pattern to which he consistently would return for *September of My Years* (1965), *Sinatra at the Sands* (1966), *Francis Albert Sinatra and Antonio Carlos Jobim* (1967), *Francis A. and Edward K.* (1968), *Ol' Blue Eyes Is Back* (1973), and *L.A. Is My Lady* (1984). In *Softly As I Leave You*, for example, the point of view continually shifts from various spectators (the " 'in' crowd of semi-invited guests sit[ting] against the wall," or "the girl" who, when she hears Sinatra's singing, finally "forgets to wonder if he's noticed her") to the musician, with the mute tucked guardedly between his knees, because he knows: "a dropped mute means a blown take. A possible explosion."

Ultimately, Cornyn shifts to Sinatra himself. Through Cornyn's words, the audience inhabits, as it were, the singer—as he readies himself: "His hands stuff into his pockets. His knees bend half an inch, like a tennis pro waiting for his opponent's best serve. He studies the microphone—friend or enemy? He fiddles with it, moving it maybe a quarter of an inch closer. He balances on the balls of his feet, his eyes feeling their way through the already memorized poetry before him." As he sings: "The action is up at the solo mike. He leans into the words with deceptively casual grace. Like a high jumper when he's loping down the gravel path to the point of no return." And when he finishes: "He looks over the top of the music stand. For the first time he has a Lucky going. He leans into the mike with the boyish pride of a kid who's just made his first bike ride around the whole block no hands." Through Cornyn's notes, the reader thus intimately experiences the action in a way most pre-MTV record buyers could only dream of: not merely in the studio or from the orchestra, but from behind the microphone as well.

Besides shifting points of view, the Reprise annotations display what would become distinctive literary mannerisms of the Stan Cornyn style: the "lavish" use of similes, motifs, repetition, and allusions. The similes, which on later albums would develop almost their own patois,[9] seem to be Cornyn's first attempts at developing a Wolfian narrative voice. With the aforementioned tennis player, the high jumper, and the boy on his bike, gone is "that pale beige tone" traditionally expected of an objective observer (Wolfe 38). In its place is a voice which tries to reflect the oxymoronic nature of Sinatra: the hard work and raw talent, the experience and innocence, the toughness and tenderness, which the singer would come to epitomize in the American popular imagination.

Within the individual annotations, Cornyn's use of motifs frequently unifies the texts. For example, in the *L.A. Is My Lady* (1984) note, entitled "'The anchovy tonight is an endangered species,'" food images predominate. From the smell of pizza in the elevator and the musicians' buffet of "chicken wings, greens, slaw, shrimp, and macaroons" to the professional jargon of "clams" and "anchovies," Cornyn details how Sinatra, Quincy Jones, and an all-star band have whipped up the "the newest Frank Sinatra Cook Book" ("Anchovy").

On *That's Life* (1966), war provides a powerful vehicle for the controlling simile.[10] "Like wars," Sinatra LPs are: "best remembered not by the issues, not by the countries, but by the havoc they create and the ingenuity of their arms makers. Havoc with brand new arms came again with 'That's Life.'" Throughout the annotation, the title track remains "the latest war," and, when describing Sinatra's performance of the song as a concert finale in Las Vegas, Cornyn concludes that it is: "a reasonable size war. Other than that not much else is happening." The bravado (and even flippancy) of such a statement cannot be overstated considering that by December 1966 some 385,000 U.S. military personnel were already in Vietnam (Kutler 555). Sinatra recordings now apparently rank as historic events.[11]

Consistent with the "New Journalism," a variety of traditional rhetorical patterns of repetition also marks the Cornyn style. In characterizing his record of "That's Life," the "ONE SONG" Sinatra went into the studio to record—despite the fact that "nobody in his right puttees goes in to record ONE SONG"—Cornyn employs alliteration, consonance, and other types of repetition in the alternately plosive and sibilant phrase: "A totally persuasive, percussive, permissive, unpassive thing." For *My Way* (1969), Cornyn's anaphoric organization can lead to only one man:[12]

> If a man moves through life . . .
> If a man grows in harmony . . .
> If you pass a man whose face looks . . .
> And if you hear a man who will only do it his way . . .
> And if you can find a man who can remember and walk and grow and
>   look in all these ways—that man is worth the listening.

And "that man," naturally, could only be Frank Sinatra.

Cornyn also packs his texts with allusions to both the current release,[13] for example, "Softly and with a grin he greets the musicians," and previous Sinatra landmarks, such as the Capitol LP *The Point of No Return* (1961). In this way, the reader is faced simultaneously with Sinatra's impressive past and still-potent present.[14] The characteristically loud drumming at the *Softly As I Leave You* sessions, for example, is a "hangover from the dance band days a couple a (*sic*) decades back." Who else is there, Cornyn's texts repeatedly ask, who still does or, for that matter, ever did it as well as Sinatra?

This appreciation for both the man and his history is captured best on *September of My Years* (1965). Here Cornyn's tone and approach, while explicitly stating the album's theme—a man's reflecting upon his past—also aim to cultivate an air of solemnity toward the stature and artistry which Sinatra's hard-fought and fully lived life has merited:

> Tonight will not swing. Tonight is for serious.
> Inside, the musicians, led by coatless, posture-free Gordon Jenkins
>   rehearse their voice-empty arrangements. Waiting for his arrival.
> Outside, in the hall, the uniformed guards wait and wonder what to
>   do with their hands.
> Unruly fiddle players, who love recording like they love traffic jams,
>   tonight
> they bring along their wives who wait to one side in black beaded
>   sweaters.

> And these wives and these fiddle players and all of these are different
> tonight. For in a few minutes a poet will begin to speak of years
> ago.

This reverent anticipation of Sinatra's advent, uttered in almost hushed
tones, is dispelled temporarily by the singer's casual entrance and easy-
going conversation. The audience's high regard of him must not, after
all, blind them to his humanity:

> He arrives. Tie-loosened, collar loosened. The guards at the studio
>   door edge out of the way.
> "Good morning, sir," he says. "Who's got the game on?"
> Thirty orchestra wives wish they had the late scores memorized. Four
>   men look around for a transistor radio.
> "Hello, Sidney, how are ye. What's happenin' in the music business?"

However, once the music commences, his joking[15] with arranger/con-
ductor Gordon Jenkins and the musicians abruptly ends (and the duly
reverent tone of the text thus returns). Jenkins is "not leading the orchestra" but "*being*" it. From the podium, he "beams down attentively,
his face that of a father after his son's first no-hitter. The wives in their
black beaded sweaters muffle their charm bracelets." A heightened, antiquated diction and a syntactically challenged sentence structure govern the remainder of the text as "this archetype of the good life . . .
graces his memory with a poet's vision":

He sings of the penny days. Of the roselipt girls and candy apple times. Of
green winds, of a first lass who had perfumed hair. April thoughts . . . He has
lived enough for two lives, and can sing now of September. Of the bruising
days. Of the rouged lips and bourbon times. Of chill winds, of forgotten ladies
in limousines.
    September can be an attitude or an age or a wistful reality. For this man it is a
time of love. A time to sing.

Besides alluding to any number of songs on the album ("It Was a Very
Good Year," "When the Wind Was Green," and the title track, for example), the note concludes with what amounts to Cornyn's lapidary
appraisal of the timelessness of Sinatra's art: "A thousand days hath
September." More than a singer, more than an artist, Sinatra becomes
in Cornyn's language an icon to be revered.
    The liner notes in which Cornyn does not follow the anticipation-
entrance-performance-appreciation pattern are even more poetic ven-
tures into fashioning a legendary Sinatra. The myth-making language

of epic, for example, fills the five columns on the inside of the gatefold cover of *Frank Sinatra: A Man and His Music*, the two-record anthology narrated by the singer in celebration of his fiftieth birthday in 1965. What begins simply with "This is the story of a lean man and his music" concludes: "Sinatra is fifty. But when he walks into a room—or into a world—there is no doubting where the focus is. It is on that singular man. On that man who stands straight on earth, sure in a universe filled with doubt. On that man, no taller than most, who came and saw and conquered." The writer, it seems, has elevated Sinatra to the apex not simply in the world of musical entertainment, but on a more epochal (and even metaphysical) plane. No longer relegated to a former generation or even to the present, Sinatra now is for the ages.

Appropriately enough, "On Sinatra or How to Be Timeless Tonight" for *Strangers in the Night* (1966), Cornyn returns to the site of one of the singer's earliest triumphs in order to juxtapose the ephemera of contemporary rock culture with the permanence of Sinatra:

Back in New York, where he started, where twenty thousand bobby soxers once pressed themselves against the doors of the Paramount Theatre to see him, things are different. The brilliant bronze doors are green with neglect. On one side wall, the chalk legend: "The Animals Are Loved Only by Girls Named Josephine."

Animals may come, and they sure do go, but Sinatra stayeth. He stays to sing. Whatever it says at the top of your calendar, that's what Sinatra sings like: 66, 67, 99 . . . He isn't with the times. More than any other he is the times.

There's no need for Sinatra to adapt to the changing times; for if, at any point, he perhaps may seem out of touch, it is only because his "honesty" renders him natural and his naturalness universal and atemporal. On *Moonlight Sinatra* (1966), even any thought of his obsolescence is illusory; he is our life's blood:

> To sing of the Moon, and not of missiles, of romance and
>   not of fudge, of love and not lollipops, is old-fashioned.
> Something out of Grandma's day. Out of date, like the stars.
> Non-chic, like Valentines. Corny, like your own heart's beat.

For *Frank Sinatra: The World We Knew* (1967), Sinatra is a force of nature:[16]

> The sun had plunged into the Pacific, somewhere southwest of
>   Bel-Air.
> In Studio One, Sinatra, like the Pacific, makes his own waves.

And, by *My Way* (1969), the solar system has become all but Sinatracentric:[17]

> If a man moves through life, walking as if he knows the planets are watching him, and might be amused by the presumption—that man is Frank Sinatra.

Vigorous but vulnerable, everyman yet Sinatra, he is no mere "saloon singer."[18] In his liner notes over the course of several years, Cornyn steadily removed Sinatra not only from the domain of the commonplace, but also from the glamorized realm of Hollywood. In its place, he created for the entertainer a cosmos of his own. The bardic lyricism of Stan Cornyn, the employee of Reprise Records,[19] was intended, of course, to sell records. He aimed at creating a marketable image for Sinatra the Franchise.[20] Nevertheless, as literary critic Robert Scholes suggests in his delineation of a "rhetoric of textual economy" in *Protocols of Reading*, advertising and poetry are far from mutually exclusive endeavors (108). Scholes invokes the categorization by semiotician Charles Morris of poetic language as "appraisive-valuative discourse" to illustrate poetry's capacity to sell an idea by making it attractively convincing (Morris 125). As Scholes writes:

Poetry exists . . . to make the bird birdy and the whale whaley, or even, as in the case of Archibald MacLeish, to make the poem poemy . . . Or as a more recent semiotic critic like Umberto Eco might put it, poems and ads exploit the same metaphoric and metonymic pathways within the network of unlimited semiosis to achieve their similar ends. (Scholes 116)

Poets, in other words, sell readers on their visions of the world by making readers see the world, even if but for a moment, just as the poets wish. This "exchange of pleasure and power" occurs at what T.S. Eliot called the "bewildering minute" when readers succumb to the authority of the writer's vision/image/sales pitch (Scholes 108). Stan Cornyn's liner notes, in the end, were successful at selling the franchise because of his ability to evoke Eliot's "bewildering minute" so consistently, to achieve again and again "the greatest single virtue of art," according to Scholes, a "change from the normal, a defense against the ever-present threat of boredom" (121). Each Sinatra album that Cornyn annotated offers a startlingly fresh view of the singer's world, from the description of the well-traveled arrangements of Count Basie and his orchestra performing live with Sinatra at the Sands in Las Vegas in 1965—Ask for 'One O' Clock Pump' and they'll bring out a sheet of music that looks like a hunk of Kleenex after a flu epidemic"—to the recording sessions for *L.A. Is My Lady* (1984)—"One of the elevators doesn't work. Everything else does."

And, for good or ill, work these liner notes did. Indeed, it might be argued that the textual Sinatra as written by Cornyn became so compelling that it began to eclipse both the man and his music as well as to encourage, at least partially, the criticism of the new, more conservative, Sinatra who arose in the seventies (Rockwell 202–211). Ralph Gleason's 1974 essay, "Frank: Then and Now," for example, sadly depicts a Sinatra larger than life and, consequently, divorced from it:

The voice is good today. Those warm tones are there and the phrasing. He can really do it like a true professional. But I don't believe anymore, that he is one of us. He's one of them now, singing from the other side of the street and I guess he doesn't even have a whiff of how power-mad and totalitarian it all seems, those bodyguards and the Rat Pack and all that egocentric trivia that has nothing at all to do with the music. (227)

No longer the voice of his audience, Frank seemingly had become someone, even something, else. Sinatra, according to critics like Gleason, had destroyed his relationship with the public by getting lost in the trappings of Cornynesque celebrity instead of remaining true to his heart, true to his art.

Of course, whether Sinatra, either the man or the artist, in actuality, had changed significantly is immaterial. The "Sinatra" genie that ad-man Cornyn helped to fashion already had been let out of its commercial bottle, and, with its "aggregate, cumulative . . . [and] almost, one might say, immanent" power, there was simply no recapturing it (Wicke 175). This dynamic is not unlike the evolution of advertising as described in Jennifer Wicke's 1988 *Advertising Fictions: Literature, Advertisement, and Social Reading.* While advertising owed its origins to literature, "the institution of advertising" quickly developed to the point that it no longer needed and even surpassed (or, at the very least, bypassed) literature: "Advertising once announced fictions—that was its job, to accompany them into the world of discourse as a mediating shield and a triumphal herald. Advertisement was the hieroglyph of fiction, until its own fictions became the book of the modern world" (Wicke 175). The relationship between Cornyn's annotations and Sinatra's albums closely parallels this description of the historical development of advertising. Originally meant only to trumpet the new Sinatra product, Cornyn's composition of a Sinatra icon soon took on a life of its own. In the final analysis, despite—and, perhaps, even due to—the excesses inherent in both the compositional strategies and rhetorical language of his annotations, Stan Cornyn contributed immeasurably to the complex iconography of Frank Sinatra. Cornyn, after all, provided the audience with precisely the confident, if somewhat prickly, image we always had desired for understanding ourselves and our place in *The World We Knew*: "Decades spent in living, in recording, and in singing small but poignant truths about loving. This ambiguous man with clear, touching insights. Sinatra at a microphone, nurturing a bouquet of emotions, then plucking them in full flower, without first checking for possible thorns."

NOTES

1. Liner notes have held a significant place on Sinatra releases at least since songwriters Sammy Cahn and Jimmy Van Heusen offered their thoughts on the back of the Capitol LP *Only the Lonely* (1958), and Ralph Gleason wrote an essay for the Capitol LP *No One Cares* (1959).

2. The self-deprecatingly comic introduction to "Eye Witness" only mentions a dozen or more liner notes for Frank Sinatra" (55). His sixteen, however, comprised the majority of Sinatra's twenty-five LPs from 1964 to 1995 (excluding compilations, soundtracks, *The Reprise Musical Repertory Theatre* albums, or other projects for which the singer only appears on some tracks). See appendix I.

3. The equating of Sinatra's and Cornyn's voices is made more manifest in the rather ambiguous final sentence of the introduction to "Eye Witness": "Stan Cornyn has tried his level best, re-creating a composite of those many nights, many sessions, many albums with many cast changes, but with one voice constant." (55). In so many ways, as this chapter will demonstrate, that constant voice was the annotator's as much as the singer's.

4. In 1963, by selling his controlling interest in Reprise, Sinatra "had at last achieved what he had originally set out to do at Capitol in 1959: run his own subsidiary label where he could call the shots and yet let someone else sign the checks. And that's without taking into consideration the millions that went into his own pockets" (Friedwald, *The Song Is You* 415–416).

5. Cornyn would annotate albums for other Reprise artists and members of the Rat Pack (e.g., Dean Martin's 1965 *Houston* and Sammy Davis Jr.'s 1966 *Sammy Davis Jr. Sings, Laurindo Almeida Plays*) but never with the same frequency or consistency as those he did for Sinatra.

6. Readers can note the indebtedness to the Cornyn style of both Gene Lees's 1967 essay on the Sinatra-Jobim sessions "The Performance and the Pain" (130–132) and Paul "Bono" Hewson's introduction of Sinatra at the 1994 Grammy Awards (213–214).

7. Gay Talese, during the mid-1960s, would publish two pieces of "New Journalism" on Sinatra. For the *New York Times*, in July 1965, he would write "Sinatra Means a Jumping Jilly's and a Lot Less Sleep for Another Cat

at His Favorite Bar," and for the April 1966 *Esquire*, the now classic "Frank Sinatra has a Cold."

8. The appreciation may be Cornyn's, the collaborators', or, as in the case of *Frank Sinatra: The World We Knew*, the singer himself: Underneath a candid photograph of Sinatra, in suit and tie, sitting on a trunk and smiling somewhat bashfully." "And then, after a time, he moves to one side. He sits down on raw wood. Listens back to his voice. And, "reacts like any man."

9. Consider, for example, "It has begun like the World Soft Champion-ships. The songs, mostly by Antonio Carlos Jobim. Tender melodies. Tender like a two-day, lobster-red Rio sunburn, so tender they'd scream agony if handled rough. Slap one of his fragile songs on the back with a couple of trumpets? Like washing crystal in a cement mixer" (Cornyn, "At Last").

10. Interestingly, it is the absence of war in the *Moonlight Sinatra* liner notes of the very same year that, in Cornyn's view, distinguishes the timeless Sinatra from the fleeting folk singers: "To sing of the Moon, and not of mis-siles, is old-fashioned."

11. Cf. "At 7 PM the orchestra, assembled here with much the same care that went into assembling the Invasion of Normandy, is ready" (Cornyn, "Anchovy").

12. Cornyn uses anaphora for *Ol' Blue Eyes Is Back*, as well: "He is maybe a bit tanner. He sings with his hands on top of the music stand . . . He sings and it's the voice. . . . He is still, no contest, the best this world knows."

13. Cornyn also alludes to or incorporates the title of the album into his notes for *September of My Years, Strangers in the Night, My Way*, and *Ol' Blue Eyes Is Back*.

14. This is a theme that Cornyn will return to again and again in the liner notes. Cf. the past-meets-present of "After All These Years" on the back of *Francis A. and Edward K.* (1968).

15. Sinatra's joking at recording sessions is stressed repeatedly by Cornyn: for example, "That was an old Chesterfield that just came up on me. Around 1947, it felt like" (1967); "Let's play some dirty songs" (1968); "I just fig-ured I'd do some work. No fun trying to hit a golf ball at eight at night" (1973); "Anybody got any oxygen?" (1984). The weakness of the humor only leads Cornyn to another conclusion about the man's power. As he writes in "On Sinatra or How to Be Timeless Tonight": "And if he tosses off a tired joke about his tired tonsils . . . If he smiles about hoping one of his kids comes along soon so he can retire . . . If he clears his throat with a line about having just swallowed a shot glass, the people all laugh. If they didn't he'd know he was in trouble. When they stop laughing, then you're in trou-ble. But Frank ain't in no trouble."

16. On *Francis A. and Edward K.*, his singing even eclipses the beauty of the roses given to Duke Ellington for his birthday; on *L.A. Is My Lady*, Sina-tra in the studio resembles a rite of spring.

17. On *Ol' Blue Eyes Is Back*, Cornyn seems to satirize his own hyperbole by quoting the "record executive" who "whispers in anticipation . . . how he wants to 'go on the road with this album and compare him . . . to Lincoln.' " It might be argued that, due to the critical distance made possible by Sinatra's two-year retirement, the writer rethought some of the immoderation of earlier notes.

18. Sinatra, on *Sinatra 80th: Live in Concert* (1995), addresses his categorization as a saloon singer in his introduction to "Angel Eyes."

19. Cornyn would become executive vice president of Warner Brothers Records (Cornyn, "Eye Witness" 55).

20. Michael Schudson describes advertising as "capitalist realism" which tries to "picture reality as it should be—life and lives worth emulating" (85). Cornyn's depiction of Sinatra, with its mixture of grandeur and humanity, certainly presents the singer as an exemplum for the audience.

CHAPTER **4**

Left Standing at *Watertown* Station: The Chairman of the Board in the Time of Woodstock

In his February 1963 *Playboy* interview, Frank Sinatra, the "acknowledged king of showbiz" (Sinatra 35), is quoted as saying:

> Whatever else has been said about me personally is unimportant. When I sing, I believe. I'm honest. If you want to get an audience with you, there's only one way. You have to reach out to them with total honesty and humility. This isn't a grandstand play on my part; I've discovered—you can see it in other entertainers—when they don't reach out to the audience, nothing happens. You can be the most artistically perfect performer in the world, but an audience is like a broad—if you're indifferent, endsville. (36)

Aside from the characteristic, and some have suggested ghostwritten, jargon, the significance of the excerpt stems from Sinatra's very clear, if metaphorical, understanding of his audience as a "broad" to be wooed, a woman to be won. For it will be this same conception of audience that informs and echoes throughout his little-known 1970 concept album, *Watertown*.

In late August 1969, grappling with the desire to adapt to the radically altered landscape of American popular music, Frank Sinatra en-

tered the studio to record what would become one of his least commercially successful albums ever. From its pop-rock pedigree (composers Bob Gaudio and Jake Holmes were both part of "The Four Seasons"
of Frankie Valli fame) to its elaborate packaging (a gatefold cover design
and thematic poster of Sinatra standing at a train station), *Watertown (A
Love Story)*, a ten-track song cycle depicting a marriage on the rocks,
seemed to offer record buyers what they wanted: a folk-rock LP that
manifested the relevance and honesty of the singer-songwriter rather
than the apparently archaic iconography of the saloon *habitue* or
"Ring-a-ding-ding" swinger. But its meager reception at the time of its
release (reaching only #101 in ten short weeks on *Billboard*'s album
chart) was regarded as proof of an artistic failure which only further suggested how out-of-step and desperate Sinatra was becoming.

Far from pandering to the youth market, however, *Watertown (A
Love Story)* showcased a vital, if conflicted, artist willing to experiment
and eager to extend the boundaries of both his music and his audience.
And some thirty years later *Watertown* still surprises by powerfully allegoriz-
ing Sinatra's career crisis of the late 1960s and early 1970s. Like the protagonist, Sinatra is anxious to win back the love of his life, the audience,
but is unsure of his ability to succeed.

The love story that the song cycle tells is a sadly simple one. The narrator is a man whose wife, Elizabeth, has left him and his two sons, Michael and Peter, rather unexpectedly and with little fanfare ("Goodbye"
1–8). She even has left Watertown, their sleepy hometown, and moved
to the city, where, as is implied only later, she has met someone else
("What's Now Is Now"). In the album's penultimate track, the husband receives a letter in which she states her intention to return ("She
Says" 15), while the final song, "The Train," depicts his anxiously waiting at the station for her to arrive. The train arrives, but the LP ends
with the listener uncertain about both the fate of their marriage and, indeed, whether Elizabeth has returned at all ("The Train" 21–27).

The song cycle, while narrative in form, is essentially elegiac in tone:
a study of distance—physical, temporal, and psychological—for the
bulk of the album portrays the unnamed narrator's attempts to grapple
with Elizabeth's departure and to understand what precisely had happened to their marriage. How had they gone from a time when they
shared the remarkable excitement of a storybook romance ("Elizabeth" 4–5) to a point now when they do not even recognize each other
("Goodbye" 20–23)? How had they grown so far apart? Had it never
been real love? Had it all been simply unreal from the beginning? Why
did they not know one another anymore?

The strength of the song cycle is its tight, if simple, construction. The single voice of the husband limits the perspective and emphasizes the uncertainty the narrator feels throughout the songs.[1] By giving only his perspective, without a clear delineation of the sources and intensity of her pain, the lyrics never allow listeners to step back and see the "big picture." The listeners are, in a sense, trapped in the same confusion and feeling of loss as the protagonist. While in the tradition of Sinatra's similarly themed ballad albums of the Capitol years, the thrust of *Watertown*—from its gatefold collage of pictures, letters, and remembrances to its sound effects—is decidedly different in both aim and design from his previous recordings. This difference can be seen in even the most minor formal detail: the sound of a train leaving.

The sound effect of Elizabeth's train leaving Watertown at the end of the first song does two things. First, it clearly marks this album as a departure from Sinatra's previous recordings. Except for the 1953 Capitol single "Rain (Falling from the Skies)," with its recording of actual falling rain, the sound effects on Sinatra's recordings are musical in nature. (The dog imitations by Donald Bain on Sinatra's 1951 Columbia duet with Dagmar, "Mama Will Bark," perhaps fall in between those two examples.) On *Watertown*, however, in the tradition of the applause on the Beatles' *Sergeant Pepper's Lonely Hearts Club Band* and other rock albums, the verisimilitude and loneliness of the train sound are necessary. The simple effect is a clarion call to record buyers: *Watertown* is like no previous Sinatra album.

Second, within the narrative structure of the album, the sound of the train's departure demands its return at the conclusion. As the train leaves the station at the end of the title track, listeners are thrown immediately and dramatically into the midst of the narrator's turmoil. And only with the husband's initial optimism in "The Train" can listeners begin to hope to escape the purgatory of waiting into which they have been cast. This train, it seems, is the only way in and out of Watertown.[2]

Gaudio and Holmes also accentuate the trapped feeling through the motif of rain on *Watertown*. Introduced immediately, in the third line of the first song, the motif recurs regularly, as if, along with Elizabeth, the sun has abandoned him and his family. In three subsequent songs ("Michael and Peter," "She Says," and during the climactic approach and departure of "The Train"), rain colors the action both at home and in the city by accentuating the darkness and solitariness of the characters' lives. The rare appearance of the sun only symbolizes what had been and what could be, although, by this point in time, he even hesitates to predict tomorrow's dawn ("Michael and Peter" 33). Dra-

matically, the sun breaks through at the beginning of the final song, as
the music swells almost joyfully in anticipation of Elizabeth's return,
only to disappear once more, before the song's and album's end. The
small town despair that hovers over Watertown from the beginning remains until the bitter end.

The music, which critics almost uniformly dismiss for its sameness,
also helps create this atmosphere of confinement. The subdued and
simple arrangements correspond perfectly to the sleepy loneliness of
the setting. And, while even a brief listening makes perfectly clear that
the album was not arranged by a Riddle, Stordahl, Jenkins, or Costa,
the resulting sound was obviously intentional and necessary. The mani-
festly different texture—epitomized by "She Says," the song Friedwald
calls "the wierdest thing . . . Sinatra ever recorded" (*The Song Is You*
442)[3]—was meant to capture the same experimental feel as on *A Man
Alone*. An album as orchestrally elaborate and polished as Sinatra's *Only
the Lonely* or *Point of No Return*, for example, only would have clashed
with the folk-rock, everyman, nature of the project. The elementary,
restrained, and, to some degree, dreary melodies, however, create and
maintain the necessary mood perfectly.

Other plot particulars also add to the texture of the narrative and understanding of the characters. The narrator's loyalty to and frustration
with his thankless job at the Santa Fe Railroad add to the claustrophobic and desperate feel of the piece ("Michael and Peter" 14–17). Unap-
preciated and overlooked at work, he always had his family before; now
even that safe haven lies in tatters. The old, confused gardener, John
Henry, who needs to be told repeatedly that Elizabeth is gone parallels
the narrator in his never fully grasping the meaning of her absence either ("Michael and Peter" 23–26). Even the difference between the
husband and wife, or at least the critical distance they have grown apart,
is underscored by their orders at the coffee shop when she says goodbye: his simple apple pie and her fancier (New York?) cheesecake
("Goodbye" 14). Given the critical commonplace of Sinatra's great
musical storytelling skill, the rich details of *Watertown*, which showcase
the carefully wrought nature of the album's storytelling, have been curiously overlooked in previous discussions of the album.

The obvious reason is that the storytelling here is of a much different
sort than earlier Sinatra concept albums. Here, the emphasis is not
simply on Sinatra's ability to make the compositions of Broadway giants
like Porter, Gershwin, and Kern, outside of their original contexts,
sound as if they are the singer's own words personally directed toward
his listeners. On *Watertown*, the songs interconnect independently of

the singer. And it is that detachment that typically has made *Watertown* the least interesting of his albums to fans and music critics. It is as if they think anyone of Sinatra's era (a Crosby, Bennett, or Como, etc.) could have made *Watertown* with little, if any, discernible differences in the end product. The error in that thinking, however, is that few of Sinatra's contemporaries were willing to experiment in the radical ways Sinatra had always done (most recently with the Jobim, Ellington, and McKuen albums of 1967–1969, for example). And it is Sinatra's willingness to experiment that makes *Watertown* uniquely his own.

It is the uncertainty of the narrator's present and his questioning of the validity of his past relationship with his audience that provide *Watertown* with a most compelling, and personal, subtext. For, if the plot is understood allegorically, as Sinatra's estrangement from an audience whom he had wooed and won some thirty years previous, only to lose them now to rock music, then *Watertown*'s ambiguous conclusion poignantly captures the singer's very immediate professional anxiety about his ability to continue to connect with the audience. While this certainly does not suggest that each detail in the plot has a direct corollary in Sinatra's life or career, it is difficult to deny that the contemporary situation of Sinatra and his audience in 1969 and 1970 closely parallels the relationship-in-transition depicted on the album. In fact, Pete Hamill already was employing the same metaphor, albeit more obliquely, on the occasion of Sinatra's retirement in 1971 when he noted that "For the past five years, Sinatra and his audience began to drift apart" (Rockwell 202).[4]

The keys to understanding the allegorical dimension of the album lie in the characterizations of the narrator's immediate family: Elizabeth and her two sons, Michael and Peter. The rather intricate characterization of the woman who abandons the man with whom she has shared her life ties her quite intriguingly to the pop-music-buying public. And the two very different products of the relationship between the artist and his audience, Michael and Peter, reflect the dual nature of the recordings Sinatra had always produced for that audience.

Elizabeth, perhaps because she exists on the album exclusively from the perspective of her husband, is an intriguingly complex and, at times, refreshingly inconsistent character. Very much like the audience of popular music, she is unpredictable, unpretentious, and ever eager to embrace the next big fad. For example, Elizabeth is depicted as an unaffected, if gullible, woman. As her husband describes her in "What a Funny Girl (You Used to Be)":

> I never met a person more sincere
> you'd always listen with an open ear
> you'd fall for lines so easily
> whatever they were selling
> you'd buy three. (14–18)

Like Elizabeth, the pop audience traditionally has favorites but, at the same time, is easily distracted and eminently suggestible.

Also similar to Elizabeth is the timidity of the pop audience in the face of nonconformity—even when the audience wants to be rebellious. (How anarchic is it, after all, for thousands at a time to don makeup at a Kiss concert or for Madonna wannabes to bare their navels *en masse*?) The real strength of these "rebellions" is, ironically, their strength in numbers. Elizabeth is no different; even as she calmly and boldly sets off to the city on her own, she worries about how she might be accepted by the people back home ("What's Now Is Now" 9–13). It is important to note that this is only the husband's hypothesis; he, in fact, does not know exactly what drove her away and naturally would like to place the blame somewhere else. Nevertheless, the parallel to the pop audience is not lessened. Did the audience give up on Frank or did he drive them away? The case can be made both ways.

The *Watertown* album itself, for example, while contemporary in so many ways, would not have been very attractive to the younger generation—given its middle-aged theme. At the same time, it was still a radical enough departure, especially as the follow-up to his Rod McKuen album *A Man Alone*, to have turned longtime fans away, as well. In short, the low sales of the album were not simply the result of fickle record buyers.

Most importantly, however, like Elizabeth, the pop audience also tends not to be terribly focused—at least, not for extended periods of time—since they always are on the lookout for something new. At any given point in time, everyone knows (and many, many people buy) the recordings of a David Cassidy, Paula Abdul, or Spice Girls because theirs are the inescapable hits of that particular point in pop music history—until the next new sensation comes along:

> You always had a thousand things to do
> getting all involved with something new
> always some new recipe
> the kitchen always looked like world war three. (6–9)

Finally, like Elizabeth, the bulk of record buyers are perennially young as well:

> You always looked a little out of place
> all grown up with freckles on your face
> we'd spend each night with company
> just you the teddy bears the dolls and me
> what a funny girl you used to be. (1–5)

In some ways, she never has grown up, and with this youthfulness comes the immaturity of running away. Nevertheless, despite the way he has been treated, despite her (from his perspective) sudden desertion, he still loves her, wants her, and needs her—as their children do, as well.

Michael and Peter, the two sons, while distinct from each other, share traits of their two parents, both individually and collectively ("Michael and Peter" 1–5). What is to be made of them in this reading? The very different, if kindred, appearances of the offspring of this relationship, if interpreted allegorically as the physical consequences of the connection between the recording artist and his record-buying audience, can be understood, without too much of a stretch, as the records that Sinatra released during his career. And certainly from the time Sinatra arrived at Capitol Records in 1953, Sinatra's output was decidedly split between the recording of singles and albums. The well-documented invention of the concept album by Sinatra, arranger Nelson Riddle, and producer Voyle Gilmore, need not be discussed again here, but it is clear that Sinatra—more so than most recording artists—unmistakably distinguished between the songs he released as singles and the recordings he made for albums such as *In the Wee Small Hours*, *Come Fly with Me*, and *Only the Lonely*. And this dichotomy continued during the Reprise years. As Will Friedwald writes, Sinatra: "inaugurated a policy of polarization between the comparatively high-brow masterpieces he continued to sweat over with Riddle, May, and Jenkins and the ephemera—often other people's hits—he knocked off to feed the jukeboxes" (*The Song Is You* 418).[5] In other words, while both shared traits, one child was more like the serious artist, while the other took after his mother, the pop audience. Sinatra always had cared about the popular music fan, the singles-buying audience, and even as Woodstock was shaking the music establishment at its core, an older Sinatra refused to give up on the possibility of selling his records to the younger generation. He had survived the aging of the 1940s bobby-soxers and became even bigger after his comeback in 1953. Who was to say he could not reconnect again? Who was to say that their marriage could not be saved?

The *Watertown* narrator is even convinced that he would not change a thing about their relationship. At the close of Side One, he is certain that, as the song's title makes clear, he "would be in love anyway." And it is this song which most demands that the album be given a broader, more autobiographical, reading than that of a simple tale of husband and wife. In *Watertown*, Elizabeth has left without explanation or promise to return, and the husband, all the while, struggles to discover the reason that she left—ever hoping against hope to win her back ("Goodbye" 24–27). The sense of abandonment that the speaker feels in the final song of the first side however cannot be underestimated, for the recording artist himself must have been feeling rather abandoned:

> If I lived the past over
> Saw today from yesterday
> I would be in love anyway
> If I knew that you'd leave me
> If I knew you wouldn't stay
> I would be in love anyway. (1–6)

While Sinatra was still making hits at fairly regular, if somewhat less than chart-topping, intervals, it was evident to everyone that a major shift in both the theory and praxis of popular music had occurred since the dawn of the rock era. Sinatra, along with every other singer of American popular standards, needed to decide how to adapt to the changing demographics of the music business.

This sea change was apparently very much on Sinatra's mind during his hiply-titled November 25, 1968, television special, "Francis Albert Sinatra Does His Thing." In his opening monologue, he speaks of the big changes the country has undergone in the brief time (two years?), since his last special; he mentions how potent and important a force the younger generation has become in politics, civil rights, and, yes, record sales. In the course of the show, consequently, Sinatra sings the contemporary "Cycles," musically salutes the history of African Americans with Dianne Carroll, and dons an appropriate costume to perform with the flamboyantly attired "The 5th Dimension." This certainly is not your mother's Frank Sinatra.

In the recording studio, Sinatra actively would court the younger audience by recording with daughter Nancy, as well as such songs as Jimmy Webb's "By the Time I Get to Phoenix" (2/12/68), Lennon and McCartney's "Yesterday" (2/20/69), and Paul Simon's "Mrs. Robinson" (2/24/69). The critical consensus suggests that his performances of these and their ilk seem noncommittal and that the results were less than the honesty he had promised his audiences in 1963. The special material of *Watertown (A Love Story)*, however, stands as Sinatra's most definitive attempt at grappling with the audience issue in the only effective way he knew—musically.

At record's end, however, the central question of whether Elizabeth, the audience, has returned remains unanswered. That Sinatra, the artist, finally felt abandoned by his lady, his audience, after the release of *Watertown* is made clear by the fact that he would record only one half of an album before retiring (i.e., what would become the "B" side of 1971's *Sinatra and Company*). An even more poignant indication of the relationship's sad fate, however, was his choice of the final song he would record during what he considered to be his last studio recording session before officially retiring in 1971 (Ackelson 14). The song, a little-known but starkly beautiful John Denver composition entitled "The Game Is Over," clearly reveals a Sinatra who feels his long love affair with his audience has, in fact, concluded:

> Time there was a time
> You could talk to me without speaking
> You would look at me and I'd know
> All there is to know.
> Days I think of you
> Remember the lies we told in the night
> The love we knew
> The things we shared
> When our hearts were beating together—
> Days that were so few
> Full of love and you
> Gone the days are gone now.

But even as he seems to bid farewell to those days once and for all, Sinatra, like the *Watertown* everyman he portrays, never fully gives up on the possibility of his love's returning, never fully stops wanting his audience back. For, not insignificantly, the other songs recorded during that "final" recording session were a pair of decidedly ephemeral duets with daughter Nancy, "Feelin' Kinda Sunday," and "Life's a Trippy Thing." As transparent attempts to duplicate the success of "Something Stupid" (number one on both the *Billboard* and *Cash Box* singles chart in 1967), the songs can only suggest that—to mix my *Watertown* metaphors a bit—while he knew the train had left the station, he could not help but hope that he could still save the marriage.

Sinatra recorded "The Game Is Over" in November 1970, but even as early as August 1969, it was becoming clear to him that the heart of his audience was beating well apart from his own. And it is this palpable sense of separation—and loss—that Sinatra mines so fully and so beautifully on *Watertown (A Love Story)*. The lifelong relationship of Sinatra and the record buying public was crumbling . . . a little too quietly and all too soon. They were drifting in two different directions. And when that happened, so Sinatra believed, it was but a short distance from Watertown to endsville.[6]

NOTES

1. One song, "Lady Day," did not make the final release, perhaps significantly because it was the only one of the songs that was not from the husband's perspective. Sinatra would release the song on *Sinatra and Company* as a salute to Billie Holiday because its title, unbeknownst to the composers, was her nickname.

2. Why the sound effect is not used again during the final song, "The Train," is an interesting question. It is as if the experimental opening to the album has already been rejected. Or it may serve as an indication that this marriage will never recover, that Elizabeth's train will never return.

3. Perhaps the only serious weakness in Friedwald's landmark study, *Sinatra: The Song Is You*, is the author's inability to hide his utter contempt for almost all rock music. As a result, he tends to overstate the flaws in Sinatra's attempts to record more contemporary works by placing almost all the blame on the works themselves. For example, it seems far-fetched to condemn Sinatra's recording of Paul Simon's "Mrs. Robinson" due to the original's being a "nonlinear assemblage of non sequiturs" (Friedwald, *The Song Is You* 437) rather than on account of how the singer's interpolation of such inside jokes as "Jilly loves you" and "How's your bird, Mrs. Robinson?" nullifies the countercultural critique of Simon's lyric. To argue that the singer had plenty of reasons not to record the song is one thing; to justify its demeaning treatment is quite another.

4. And it is the persona Sinatra adopts for *Watertown* that makes the album more successful artistically than his previous effort, *A Man Alone*, which was more financially successful. Although Roger Gilbert, in his article "The Swinger and the Loser: Sinatra, Masculinity, and 50s Culture," argues that the singer shares much with the ethos of the Beats, I find that McKuen's transformation of Sinatra in 1969 into a Jack Kerouac, who had traveled innumerable roads, just could not be believed. (Of course, this failure could stem directly from McKuen's not being Kerouac.) Nevertheless, as Allen Ginsberg himself had suggested in poems such as "Las Vegas: Verses Impro-

vised for El Dorado H.S. Newspaper" (720), Sinatra was clearly a man of another generation and for the population at large to imagine him in terms of the Beats or other such countercultural figures was too much of a stretch. On the other hand, to see the singer as a man with a wife and children struggling to make life meaningful offered a more natural, and credible, fit.

5. In his liner notes to the 1996 *Capitol Singles Collection*, "Songs for Swingin' Singles: An Appreciation," Friedwald would revise this statement by discussing how, in many ways, Sinatra had been doing the same thing since his days at Capitol when his approach to recording singles was quite different from his album sessions (Friedwald, "Songs for Swingin' Singles" 4–7).

6. Further evidence of his identification of the audience as a lover is his choice to release, on his comeback album *Ol' Blue Eyes Is Back*, a song about second chances, "Let Me Try Again," while deciding against another song recorded during the same 1973 sessions, "Walk Away." It seems quite clear that the song's sentiment was simply out of sync with the way he was feeling about his audience once again.

CHAPTER 5

Strolling among the Stars: Gordon Jenkins's Reflections on Frank's Future

Long before he had himself flown to the moon with Count Basie in 1964 and dedicated an entire album, 1966's *Moonlight Sinatra*, to Earth's only natural orbiting satellite, Frank Sinatra already had taken several trips back and forth to the stars in his songs.[1] In 1940, he had "Shake[n] Down the Stars" with Tommy Dorsey and even offered his listeners solid advice in 1949's "If You Stub Your Toe on the Moon." But his having gotten "Lost in the Stars" in both 1946 and 1963 (not to mention nearly being killed in a space flight scam as "Rocky Fortune" in the eponymous 1953–1954 murder mystery radio show) might have served as fair warning to him. It clearly did not. Consequently, in 1979, when he once again returned to a space-themed composition in *The Future: Reflections on the Future in Three Tenses* by Gordon Jenkins (1910–1984), Sinatra found himself faced with a fair amount of trouble in the heavens. For while navigating his protagonist to a number of interesting destinations, the composer has "Frank" off-course for most of the trip.

The Future: Reflections on the Future in Three Tenses, the final disk of the 1979 Reprise album *Trilogy*, is both the most individualized and yet one of the least personal pieces that Sinatra ever recorded. Composed especially for the singer by longtime arranger-conductor Gordon Jenkins as the finale to Sinatra's ambitious attempt to unite songs of the past, present, and future into a three-record album, the eight songs of the musical suite focus on two basic themes. The first theme, Frank's identity, centers on Sinatra's biography and specific wishes, including at least one final trip to both his hometown of Hoboken, New Jersey, and Las Vegas, Nevada ("Before the Music Ends"), whereas the second theme, the look of tomorrow, embraces broadly futuristic concepts such as space travel ("What Time Does the Next Miracle Leave?") and vaguely philanthropic aspirations such as world peace ("World War None" and "Song Without Words"). While the suite seems not to the liking of most fans—one even calling *Trilogy* "two-thirds of a great album and a Frisbee"—the piece fails primarily because the character and *raison d'être* of "Frank," the protagonist, while alternately self-deprecating and bombastic, is more often than not surprisingly fuzzy. Despite the ability of the audience to recognize and appreciate the composer's effort in incorporating firsthand knowledge of Sinatra into the suite, listeners never quite get the singer's sense of himself on the verge of his seventieth year. In short, unlike 1965's intimate portrait *September of My Years*, *The Future* sounds surprisingly distant and artificial.

This awkward distance becomes apparent in the very start of the suite. The opening song, "What Time Does the Next Miracle Leave?" begins with the singer's self-introduction. But before he even can complete his three names, a fifty-member chorus enters and finishes it for him. "Francis Albert Sinatra" clearly has become too much of a brand name for any single man to handle. Whether such intensive choral participation stems from Jenkins's uncertainty of the singer's ability to carry the composition himself (although this seems unlikely given Sinatra's strong performances on records one and two of *Trilogy*) or simply Jenkins' need to establish, from the start, that this suite intends to capture the fullness of the singer's import is unclear. Either way, the grand scale of the orchestration and vocal arrangement tends to undercut more than highlight this assertion of Sinatra's cultural significance. When Frank takes off on a trip through the solar system, any lucid argument for his place in the future of American society—musical or otherwise—seems remote.

In the course of the record, listeners learn not a little about "Frank," the types of details that fans normally must turn to biographies and magazine profiles to discover. Jenkins, for example, offers insight into some of Frank's favorite things: Puccini, Verdi, Schubert, and Beethoven are among his preferred classical composers; Black Jack is his favorite game of chance; and his choice of pizza is cheese. Listeners also pick up on the nicknames of some of Sinatra's buddies: "Chester" for Jimmy Van Heusen, "Sarge" for Irving Weiss, and even "Lefty" for Jenkins himself. But, musically speaking, the most telling detail emerges when Jenkins celebrates Sinatra's love of conducting, something he would do on eight different albums between 1945 and 1983, for both himself and others (such as singers Peggy Lee, Dean Martin, and Sylvia Syms, as well as trumpeter Charles Turner). All these details, however personal as they may be, lack a clear focus; they simply do not add up to a convincing portrait of the man or his future.

But if Frank's role in the future is rather ill-defined, so is the future itself, which, as presented throughout the suite, is a contradictory mix of technology, ancient mythology, and magic. The planetary stops depicted in "What Time Does the Next Miracle Leave?" for example, are primarily lighthearted puns on the mythological roots of the planets' names. On Venus, named for the Roman goddess of love, spring and romance will be in the air. On Uranus, whose name derives from *Ouranos*, a Greek sky god, Frank is certain it will be heaven for the remarkably inconsequential reason that he will be greeted there with wine and pizza. Meanwhile, Jenkins puns upon the name of Pluto, the Roman god of the underworld, for both its eschatological and criminal implications. The farthest planet, after all, is filled with Frank's former associates who comically refer to their doing things his way. Thus, even as Frank attempts to soar through a heavenly future, he seems to be dragged again and again back down to a rather pedestrian Earth by both his simple tastes and his past.

Is this, however, the point at which Jenkins's composition is driving: that "Frank's" somewhat anachronous and imperfect lifestyle will never go out of fashion, that *his* way will always be *the* way? One might be tempted to assume so if it were not for the fact that the piece's vision of the future is so confusing. Its depiction of tomorrow is never clear enough to rally around or rail against. An argument in favor of a seemingly passé approach to living—the kind, for example, offered in Bill Zehme's 1997 *The Way You Wear Your Hat: Frank Sinatra and the Lost Art of Livin'*—demands some clearly defined lifestyles to which Sinatra's can offer a viable and preferable alternative. Jenkins's suite, however, presents no distinct image of what the future offers, and what is described is no less "old hat" than its depiction of "Frank."

The composer's future, despite all its space-age elements, is decidedly antiquated. In the first part of the tripartite song "The Future," for example, after Frank's return from his tour of the nine planets and his building of a desert bonfire in preparation for the peace of "World War None," the chorus of "men" and "girls" (an oddly anachronistic dichotomy in itself) seek a gypsy to discover what awaits them. The predictions, which include nothing that "they don't already know," are vague, simplistic, and straight out of B-movies: "rockets, spaceships, computers, inventions, little buttons you can push." The diction of the libretto here is simply too general: from the prehistoric club to papyrus to the television remote control, at what point in the past or present have "inventions" not been an integral part of everyday life? Such generic terms offer the listeners no convincing image upon which to hang the rest of the suite.

Nonetheless, when "given a choice," Frank rejected even these vague futuristic tools and chose instead a "magic wand," the conductor's baton, which he would use to produce music from the "enchanted maze" of instruments. While this rejection is not meant to date Sinatra—since his preference for live orchestral music to multitracking and overdubbing was well known and greatly admired—"magic wands," "enchantment," and gypsies tend to undermine Jenkins's vision of the future by utilizing language that is inconsistent with, if not downright hostile to, the concept of scientific inquiry, the driving force behind the concepts of progress and the future since the Enlightenment. By thus refusing to delineate in his libretto how progress, technological or otherwise, will benefit "Frank" (or vice versa), Jenkins offers listeners little upon which to base their appreciation of the singer or his songs. He is just a saloon singer in space, not unlike James Darren's character, Vic Fontaine, in the *Star Trek* spin-off, *Deep Space Nine*.

Without a doubt, Jenkins's composition is at its best the more it abandons the transparent dimensions of the futuristic theme. The best song of the entire suite, "I've Been There," for example, offers the protagonist as someone who has been around and who is willing to offer advice about love to the young, in much the same spirit as the speaker in Rodgers and Hammerstein's "Hello, Young Lovers." Unfortunately these insights are characterized, in the choral prelude, not simply as those of an experienced man, but also, to some extent, those of the future itself. (Luckily, the listener can forget this premise once the song proper commences.)

The song's speaker is older and no longer in the thick of romance, but, as Jenkins's title suggests, he knows precisely what the couple is experiencing (the tension, the elation, the confusion, and the hurt of love) because he too has experienced them. The strength of the song, however, (and what keeps it from being a mere retread of "Hello, Young Lovers") is its recognition of the power and omnipresence of Sinatra's music. The song avoids simply being a recapitulation/commemoration of Sinatra's infamous loves and losses; it is a celebration of the way his songs have played a major role in twentieth-century love. As Frank sings, it is as if his whole catalogue of recordings has been the soundtrack of the century, as if he himself had been there as the countless romances of countless couples have played out—not in person, but in the music that was playing in the background. As the title makes clear: he always has been there through his songs.[2] Therefore, instead of falling into the predictable pattern of revisiting the singer's past with Nancy, Ava, Mia, et alia, the song underscores the role Sinatra's music will continue to play in a very recognizable future filled with young lovers.[3]

Consequently, Sinatra's significance, which seems so undermined by all the futuristic trimmings that pervade other songs of the suite, is highlighted successfully here by Jenkins's understatement of it. With little fanfare (though with a bit of the orchestral bravado that had become synonymous with Sinatra at least since "My Way"), Jenkins reveals how Frank's music will act not only as the soundtrack of love in the future, but also how it will become the very paradigm for lovers by offering to assist them in imagining their own futures. This will be Sinatra's potent legacy: in the future, his love songs will serve to shape the experience of love not merely reflect it. Jenkins's song, in fact, succeeds in highlighting the prominent place of Sinatra within the traditions of love and courtship in a way that Sinatra's own 1976 reworking of Barry Manilow's hit "I Write the Songs" into "I Sing the Songs" fails. It captures his preeminence without sounding hubristic; it tells the truth without making Sinatra seem presumptuous. As Manilow himself quite simply suggests in his 1998 tribute, "One Man in a Spotlight," it is now impossible to imagine a time when Sinatra's music was not or will not be there.

In the very next song, "The Future (Conclusion)," however, Jenkins undercuts the universality that he has just established for Sinatra's art by having Frank wish that (unfettered by the barriers of nationality, race, or class) a musical composition of his own might be comprehensible to all. Of course, such a wish, as is the desire for world peace in "World War None," is a noble one. But it contradicts one of the most obvious truths about music, be it pop or opera: that music is indeed a universal language, that a good song need not be limited by political or economic boundaries, as suggested by the 1960 Vic Aragon drawing "Frank Sinatra Goes Latin" or Tom Russell's 2001 "When Sinatra Played

Juarez." It hardly would be a bold statement to claim that the French, Germans, Russians, and Spaniards, as well as commoners and royalty throughout the world (all of whom Jenkins mentions in the song), have enjoyed and, most probably, already have comprehended Frank Sinatra's singing, even if they had no English.[4]

Why then this superfluous wish to reach everyone? The answer is simply and pragmatically as the lyrical cue for "Song Without Words," the second instrumental in the suite. But whereas Jenkins tied the first "orchestral interlude" to Sinatra's career-long love of conducting, this piece lacks a convincing motivation—other than as a way to conclude "The Future." Balancing voice and instrumentation, of course, is a serious concern for any composer of a longer musical work, but to deny Sinatra's well-recognized international influence repudiates the very power of his art that "I've Been There" celebrates. All in all, a longer wordless song might have served the suite better.

Nevertheless, as the most ambitious composition ever written for Sinatra, *The Future* deserves special attention. Indeed, merely as the conclusion of *Trilogy*, *The Future* merits more regard than it usually receives since, as a whole, *Trilogy* is a remarkable work even in so remarkable a recording career as Sinatra's. By tackling the music of yesterday, today, and tomorrow, Sinatra seized the opportunity to identify himself officially as the premier interpreter of twentieth-century popular music. While not entirely successful, Sinatra's aim was both admirable and justified. After all, who but Sinatra deserves the title? And, in 1979, when the recording careers of his generation seemed to be all but finished, who but Sinatra could have attempted such a large-scale project? *The Future*, despite its flaws, simply cannot be dismissed by serious critics of Sinatra.

The Future, in its representation of a singer who needs to look back even as he looks ahead, offers occasional glimpses of Sinatra's significance. When its gaze tends toward a rather nondescript future, *The Future* too often gets lost in the vastness of its topic. But when it lingers upon the place of Sinatra's music in the past, present, and future lives of his listeners, the suite begins to reveal the impact Sinatra had on our notions of what it means to fall in love and the hold that his musical legacy had on the popular imagination.

NOTES

1. In the Warner Brothers Records press release for the soundtrack album for *Space Cowboys*, the 2000 film about aging astronauts in space, Clint Eastwood, producer and star, is quoted as saying: "We had to use Sinatra and

Basie's 'Fly Me to the Moon.' That was kind of a no-brainer." The sound-track also includes country and jazz versions of "Young at Heart," "The Best Is Yet to Come," and "The Second Time Around," all songs made famous by Sinatra.

2. Jenkins's lyrics simultaneously invoke both of the released covers to the 1956 *Songs for Swingin' Lovers*, on which a young couple embraces in front of a large image of Sinatra. In the more common version, Sinatra knowingly looks on as the couple hugs, while in the alternate version, a singing Sinatra has his face turned away. As both covers suggest, Sinatra has been right where the couple is now: as lover *and* soundtrack.

3. A slightly twisted example of this "Sinatra-song-as-blueprint-for-romance" concept occurred on a January 2001 episode of *Ally McBeal*. Both Peter MacNicol's John Cage, who is a bundle of nervous ticks and idiosyncratic movements and noises, and Anne Heche's Melanie West, who suffers from Tourette Syndrome, discover yet another common bond in the Sinatra father-daughter duet, "Somethin' Stupid." As they dance to Vonda Shepherd's performance of the song, John admits he always dreamed that he was singing to Nancy, while Melanie confesses that she used to imagine singing it with Frank. That this recording, which Reprise executives considered "odd" due to its incestuous subtext (Taraborrelli 362), best captures John and Melanie's close affinity for one another only underscores the unconventionality of their romance. (The familial history of the song also dovetails with a subplot about Melanie's relationship with her homeless father.)

Another variation of a Sinatra erotic paradigm is offered in Steely Dan's "Janie Runaway" (2000) in which Donald Fagen suggests a scenario right out of 1959 with Janie playing a showgirl while he takes the Sinatra role.

4. This exact point is made in Raul Nuñez's 1984 Spanish novella *Sinatra* (discussed below in Chapter 7), in which Antonio (aka Frankie), the down-on-his-luck night porter, phones into a Barcelona radio station to request a Sinatra song. Even though "he spoke no English . . . he understood every word" (9).

PART II

"SAD-EYED SINATRAS" IN SONG AND STORY

CHAPTER 6

"You Will Be My Music": Sinatra in Popular Song from the 1940s to a New Millennium

Why would forty-one garage bands in 1993 record Sinatra songs and release them in a two-disc set entitled *Chairman of the Board*? What possibly could bands named "Screeching Weasel," "Indian Bingo," "Lotion," and "Zonic Shockum" find in music that a performer from a very different time began recording in a seemingly distant world? The answer for them is exactly the same as for so many musicians before them: an immediately recognizable image with seemingly infinite possibilities for symbolism. In covering the "songs made famous by Frank Sinatra," albeit in radically different (and, some have argued, emphatically unlistenable) interpretations, these bands draw upon the same inspiration that others, from the Big Band era to the age of grunge, have for their own music. Since the first wave of Sinatra's popularity in the early 1940s, pop, rock, folk, blues, and country songwriters have found a fertile field in the lyrical and conceptual possibilities offered by "Frank Sinatra." Serving as everything from a perceived romantic rival to the symbol of American commercialism and imperial arrogance, Sinatra has offered lyricists an appropriate reflection for their musical statements. Sometimes nostalgic memory, sometimes bitter rebuke, often musical homage, they all acknowledge the man and the enduring legacy of his music.

Even as early in the singer's career as 1945, Sinatra was of such standing to serve as a cultural benchmark in the Sunny Skylar song, popularized by Benny Goodman and his orchestra, "Gotta Be This or That."[1] The song—a litany of ontological, moral, natural, and economic dichotomies—offers Frank as the sole possible counterpoint to the musical juggernaut then known as Bing Crosby, who had originally inspired Sinatra to become a singer.

In many ways, the lyric accurately reflects the reality of the music business of the time. Crosby had dominated the charts since going solo in 1931; hit songs such songs as "Brother, Can You Spare a Dime?" (1932), "Love in Bloom" (1934), "You Must Have Been a Beautiful Baby" (1938), "Swingin' on a Star" (1944), and, of course, "White Christmas" (1942) made him the preeminent pop singer. He even has been rated as the "most popular recording artist during the period 1890–1954 on the basis of his chart success" (Brackett 35). This dominance is made manifest in the Sammy Cahn-penned "Dick Haymes, Dick Todd, and Como," a V-Disc parody of "Sunday, Monday, or Always" on the rivalry among the younger singers that admits to there being but one Crosby. While all three of the singers mentioned in the title are vying with Sinatra, according to the song, no one could even hope to rival the "Old Groaner." Sinatra's arrival as a solo act in 1942, on record, on radio, and in film, however, would usher in a new era in pop music, one in which Bing finally would face real, if amicable,[2] competition, one pitting Crosby's "well-entrenched image of the 'American Everyman'" with Sinatra's edgier urban character (Brackett 61).

The friendly and good-humored nature of the competition is captured well during an appearance by Crosby's four sons on both Armed Forces Radio's "Command Performance" (March 11, 1945) and "Songs by Sinatra" (September 12, 1945). The skit written for Crosby's sons, given the commercial competition between the two singers, focuses on the necessarily secretive nature of their visit with Sinatra, Gary Crosby's comic imitation of the two singers' styles, and the dire warnings Crosby has given his four sons about Sinatra's success. The most comic mileage is gained on this last element by combining the economic pressure the elder singer feels from Frank's record sales—Bing has been burying Sinatra records in his garden the past few seasons!—with the younger singer's oft-mocked thinness. When the youngest Crosby, Lindsey, asks to see Sinatra's kitchen or wherever he has been putting all the bread and butter he's been taking out of the

Crosbys' mouths, Gary replies that surely their dad must have been lying: "Just take a look at Mr. Sinatra; you can tell he's never had a piece of bread in his life."

It is this same commercial competition of cornering the market that the Sinatra reference assumes in "Gotta Be This or That."[3] The rhyming of Sinatra's first name with a financial institution, as well as with the ominous fiscal connotations of an empty check (particularly with memories of the depression still very fresh in most people's minds), carries with it a recognition of the economic force that the Crosby-Sinatra tandem wielded. Aside from this pair, for millions of fans and the record companies, there was no one else. It was, essentially, Bing, Frank, or nothing at all.[4]

Country great Merle Travis[5] also lampoons the incredible marketability (and marketing success) of the young Sinatra in his "So Round, So Firm, So Fully Packed," which he recorded and released in 1947. The title takes the commercial slogan for the Lucky Strike brand of cigarettes, the sponsor of Sinatra's radio show in 1945–1947, applies it to a woman, and by doing so only underscores Sinatra's commercial appeal, for Sinatra already had become quite the brand name himself. In plugging Lucky Strikes during his show, for example, he frequently also branded himself as merchandise for sale by the parallel construction of his tagline, "This is FS for LS."

In his song, Travis emphasizes the commercial hold that Sinatra, the product and pitchman, had on the unassuming consumer with the twisted rhyme of "drink," "Frank," and "bank":

> Like a barfly goes for drink
> Like a bobbysoxer goes for Frank
> And just like Jesse James would go
>   for money in the bank.

Sinatra thus represents an irresistible temptation to the consumer (derided here as dissipated, immature, or, at best, just plain greedy). In any case, Frank means "money in the bank" for the manufacturer. At the same time, however, the song implies, as the Columbus Day riots and all the journalistic ink spilled over the actions, motives, and "meaning" of the bobby-soxers also suggested,[6] "Frank Sinatra" embodied a threat to civilized American men and women everywhere as dangerous as alcoholism, mob rule, or robbery. In the song, Sinatra thus becomes the two faces of capitalism: on the one hand, the product that possesses wide appeal and, to some degree, reflects the liberating nature of American equality and, on the other, the exploitative exercise of mass marketing that cynically creates and then fills a need among the populace.

A similar recognition of the dangerous attraction the bobby-soxers had toward Sinatra, and, consequently, the threat to hearth and home that he represented, is dramatized in T-Bone Walker's 1946 "Bobby Sox Blues." In the song, the voice and image of Frank so distract the singer's wife and, consequently, so disturbs their life together, that he threatens to end their marriage. She no longer cleans, cooks, or fulfills any of her other domestic responsibilities. Instead, her days are spent hunting autographs, compiling scrapbooks, and writing fan mail, to the point that T-Bone fears she no longer even recognizes him. For the blues singer, Frank thus represents direct competition, but not one that can be fought man-to-man. It is man against an image and voice seen and heard so often through a variety of media that they crowd out of her consciousness everything else. In fact, according to the song, Sinatra so dominates her thoughts and life that, when Walker asks her if she loves him, she only wonders how the singer himself would react.

The attention the songwriters gave Frank in the mid-1940s faded along with Sinatra's career and would not return in earnest until the 1970s.[7] During the 1950s and 1960s, while Sinatra references still appeared in special lyrics of older songs (for example, Bing Crosby and Rosemary Clooney's 1958 duet on Burton Lane and Ralph Freed's "How about You?" or Connie Francis's 1964 recording of "Will You Still Be Mine?"), Sinatra's post-comeback ubiquity on the charts, in films, and on television perhaps made others' references to him redundant, at best.[8] But the more significant reason for the lack of Sinatra references in new songs was certainly the rise of rock and roll and the clear declaration by its singers of the arrival of a completely unprecedented kind of, and era in, music. (Chuck Berry, remember, tells no less a musical touchstone than Beethoven to roll over!) Not surprisingly, the new music chose to ignore such forebears of popular musical hysteria as Sinatra and, by doing so, proclaimed its singularity. To the rock and roll generation, since their musical idiom was unlike anything that existed before, no one like Elvis or the Beatles could have appeared previously either. Their music, to their mind, was indeed *sui generis.* Consequently, a collective amnesia overtook several generations, for only a more mature form could recognize predecessors without perceiving them as threats.[9] By the 1980s and 1990s, however, Sinatra and his music began to accrue more and more meaning for new generations of musicians.[10]

The rock band Cracker, for example, in their serio-comic 1992 "Teen Angst (What the World Needs Now)," seeks not the original but an updated version of Sinatra. While the band clearly recognizes (and envies) Sinatra's seductive power—especially when compared to the inadequacy of the ubiquitous folk singer—they clearly demand someone new who, possessing an erotic authority similar to Frank's music, could help in orchestrating a successful sexual conquest.

Folk singer Loudon Wainwright III, meanwhile, invokes Sinatra as the ultimate headliner. In his comic 1993 "TSMNWA," an acronym for "They Spelled My Name Wrong Again," the singer, while complaining of the endless orthographic attacks on his own name, bluntly states that, if such an error ever happened to Frank: "Sinatra would have a shit fit." The humor of Wainwright's reference, of course, stems from the juxtaposition of Sinatra's entertainment clout (i.e., his ability to ensure that such an insulting mistake as a misspelled poster or marquis would never happen) with the folk singer's apparent inability to stop even serial occurrences. For Wainwright, Sinatra therefore represents true stardom and the proper treatment a celebrity should be accorded, while the songwriter submits himself in our stead, generally unrecognized if not entirely anonymous.

And, by the late 1990s, Sinatra's presence had managed to become simultaneously so universal and so nonthreatening that different musicians increasingly could invoke him entirely on their own terms. Thus, actor John Lithgow, on his children's album, *Singin' in the Bathtub*, could interpolate the singer in the 1929 title song and encourage youngsters to become little Sinatras (if only while bathing). Barry Manilow, on "Here's to the Man"[11] (the second of two original songs that frame the twelve Sinatra songs on *Manilow Sings Sinatra*), could highlight his indebtedness to Frank by alluding to his own 1976 hit "This One's for You." And the Australian band Smudge could continue, according to its website, its "fascination with all things Hank [Sinatra]" with their *Real McCoy Wrong Sinatra* album, the title of which simultaneously assumes and then immediately rejects the Sinatra who comes most readily to mind.

All of this interest makes clear why it would be a musician of the stature of Van Morrison who would make one of the earliest and (as it so happens) one of the fullest references to Sinatra in a popular song. (Lou Reed briefly would mention his attraction to both Sinatra and his daughter in the live version of the Velvet Underground's "New Age" in 1969.) In fact, in "Hard Nose the Highway," the title track of his 1973 album, Morrison invokes Sinatra as a role model, both musically and personally. Clearly drawn to the older singer for his musical abilities and his sense of survival, Morrison pays homage to Sinatra in what amounts to an anthem of knowing how to succeed in life—although not so obviously at first. The opening of the song finds Morrison apparently appreciating Sinatra's singing:

> Hey kids dig the first takes
> Ain't that some interpretation
> When Sinatra sings against
> Nelson Riddle Strings
> Then takes a vacation

But what is the listener to make of Sinatra's "vacation" at the end of the verse? Is this a criticism by Morrison of a lazy performer, an artist who attempts single takes of songs then goes on holiday? Only by song's end does it become clear to the careful listener that Morrison, far from criticizing the singer, truly is impressed that Sinatra, both in and out of the studio, has lived a life knowing exactly when to step up and when to hold back. The "vacation" reference is not to Frank on a Mediterranean cruise, but to the familiar Sinatra technique of hanging behind the beat and catching up later in a musical line. At the same time, Sinatra epitomizes for the Irish singer/songwriter an artist and man who has endured, who has managed to withstand adversity and overcome it. Sinatra more than anyone illustrates the final verse:

> Put your money where your mouth is
> Then we can get something going
> In order to win you must be prepared to
>   lose sometime
> And leave one or two cards showing

More than any other singer, Sinatra, as he came out of retirement in 1973, seemingly had weathered several careers even as he was about to embark on yet another.[12]

The "hard times" and "bad lines" of the song's chorus thus call to mind Sinatra's various struggles, personal and professional, while recognizing the singer's success in overcoming all of them, as the song's title suggests, by putting his nose to the grindstone.[13] Sinatra's "first takes" and "vacation" therefore serve Morrison not as signs of sloth or indolence, as perhaps first implied, but rather as the results of a hard-fought life and career which can then, in turn, give rise to those remarkable Sinatra interpretations.

A comparable approach by a younger musician to the meaning of Sinatra's life and music is the Soulvitamins' 1993 "If I Were Frank Sinatra," which pits the "forever hip" crooner against "a skinny white boy" whose only remedy for "this world of ills" is "the funk." Even mimicking the "Doo Bee Doo Bee Do" of Sinatra's "Strangers in the Night," the song presents a Sinatra who has it all: friends, money, a "palatial penthouse suite," and women. The young man, on the other hand, loves his "beautiful, stingray bass" since no woman would "kiss [his] ugly face." The intriguing dimension of this lyric is the ignorance of Sinatra's history that it, at first, conveys. The speaker in the song appears unaware that, in many ways, Sinatra was the archetypal "skinny white boy" who made his way to the top of the entertainment world. Nevertheless, having set up Sinatra as a paragon of material success, the song shifts gears by posing a question to the listener: "What are you looking for?" If all the listener wants is "more," perhaps only to live like Sinatra, then the listener surely will be disappointed because the singer knows that there will never be another Sinatra. What the young man does possess, however, what does matter, is his own music, the true "object of [his] affection."

This declaration of what should count—namely, true love—necessarily returns the listener to the fact that Sinatra, as distant as he may look in his palatial surroundings, is "forever hip." And his hipness must stem directly from his music, the real object of his affections. In short, all that separates the "skinny white boy" from "Frank Sinatra" are the material objects that large amounts of money can buy. Deep down they share a passion that cannot be bought or sold. That kinship, their music (as different as their two styles might be), unites them. Far from an ironic comparison, therefore, the song acknowledges Sinatra's authenticity, his dedication to his music . . . even amidst great distractions.[14] In the end, the music matters to both of them.

And it is, not surprisingly, most often to the music of Sinatra that songwriters turn for their own songs.[15] Whether it is a reference to a specific recording, such as his singing of "Stormy Weather" in Cake's 1996 "Frank Sinatra," or a more general allusion to Sinatra's music, as in Michael Veitch's 2000 "Frank Sinatra," Stephen Bishop's 1976 "On and On," Marillion's 1987 "Sugar Mice," Natasha's Ghost's 1995 "Hang Sinatra," Crowded House's 1991 "She Goes On," or even the Beach Boys' unreleased "It's Over Now" from 1977, Sinatra's records often act as the musical score for the action of the song, as a way of setting a mood and creating atmosphere.

On his *Southern Girl* album, for instance, folksinger Michael Veitch employs the pain so powerfully reflected in Sinatra's recordings as the ultimate soundtrack for a variety of life crises, including drug-induced traffic fatalities and cancer.[16] More often than not, however, Sinatra's songs are the music of love's labors lost.

Thus, in "On and On," a heartbroken lad who has just seen "his woman kissing another guy . . . puts on Sinatra / and starts to cry." Clearly alluding to one of Sinatra's classic "saloon song" albums (e.g., *In the Wee Small Hours of the Morning, Only the Lonely,* or *All Alone*), Sinatra's name and music legitimize the song's depiction of sadness as well as the concept of consolation offered by music and tears. Similarly in "Sugar Mice," the song's speaker, on the road in Milwaukee and separated from his love, tries to figure out where the relationship went wrong. Lying on his hotel bed, he hears "Sinatra calling [him] through the floorboards." The jukebox playing the Sinatra tune is "crying in the corner." Again, the rock lyricist employs Sinatra's name metonymically for the pain of loss and heartbreak, a hallmark of Sinatra's ballads.

Similarly, the California-based alternative band Natasha's Ghost suggests that the role of Sinatra's music (with a gin chaser) in dealing with heartbreak is so central that they can even suggest replacing the moon with Sinatra in their "Hang Sinatra." Consequently, what the title would seem at first to imply, namely, a dismissal of Sinatra and his music, winds up a confirmation of the unparalleled meaning and efficacy of his art.[17]

The Beach Boys, on "It's Over Now," take it a step further. Songwriter Brian Wilson turns to Sinatra not only as a musical exemplar or even as a facilitator of his pain, but as a true source of its cure: by listening—and inevitably by crying—his sadness goes away. Sinatra's songs, and, perhaps, only Sinatra's songs, can effect such a catharsis. Consequently, for Wilson, they assume an aesthetic dimension uncommon for pop music while ordaining Sinatra, in critic Edmund Santurri's words, the "musical high priest of *eros*" (199).[18]

The quasi-sacred combination of tears and Sinatra music is evoked especially effectively in Crowded House's "She Goes On." The song, an elegy, by the Australian band mourns the passing of a woman, whose first meeting with the lyricist was made more memorable by Sinatra's music. The designation of a Sinatra recording, even an unspecified one, offers the situation—especially when it becomes clear that love and marriage ensued—a traditionally romantic picture with children and a mountain setting that seems to share more with an earlier age than with 1991. This time-warping effect is compounded by the distancing that occurs in the shift in personal pronouns at this same point in the lyric. The first person plural suddenly becomes the third, as if the woman's death has destroyed utterly both the union that they shared and, at least temporarily, the recognition that he truly was her partner in this love. For only by song's end, with the repetition of the chorus, are they joined once again in eternity.

Despite these disconnections, the choice of Sinatra is telling. Sinatra's music, as opposed to that of another more contemporary artist, offers lyricist Neil Finn a pop cultural counterpart that comes closest to continuing on like the spirit of the departed. While a more topical or fashionable choice, would have only emphasized the transience of life, the Sinatra name embodies the closest thing to immortality that popular music has offered.

This same longevity, embodied in Sinatra's recording of "Stormy Weather," contributes to Cake's haunting "Frank Sinatra." Conjuring up a "faintly glimmering radio station" which sends its "ancient" signal throughout the universe, the 1996 song offers an almost apocalyptic vision of "dismembered constellations" and "flies and spiders get[ting] along together." In it, Sinatra's art is contrasted with the ephemeral nature of "your flowers of flaming truth" and "your latest ad campaigns." Just as an "ancient radiation" can be heard across the light years to the present, the present continues to transmit its own signals to the future. Sinatra's "Stormy Weather,"[19] which continues to play (and transmit) seemingly forever, thus represents something lasting, something to which we may cling amidst an utterly disposable culture (itself symbolized by both the "old man [who] . . . saves what others throw away" and the technological obsolescence inherent in the "old skipping record").

A similar convergence of past and present, which perhaps lies at the core of Sinatra music in the age of rock and roll, is tapped in both the Dream Academy's "Life in a Northern Town" and the "big band" approach of The Brian Setzer Orchestra's "September Skies." In their 1985 song, the Dream Academy, after eliciting the simple life of the town in the title, recalls the music of the early Sinatra and its ability to transport the listener elsewhere. In the second stanza, an unnamed man tells anyone in the vicinity of those turbulent early 1960s: the Kennedy assassination and the dawn of Beatlemania. At song's end, with all in tow, he heads to the train station and departs.

The cryptic nature of the song's narrative conveys a sense of change. Clearly, the world did not halt in 1963, and, as a result, we all have been forced to confront consistently a sense of a lost innocence. The designation of the recordings of a more youthful Frank conjures up an even more innocent age, one in which right and wrong were easier to differentiate and in which good always seemed to triumph over evil. Nineteen sixty-three, of course, would change all that: the buoyant exuberance of Kennedy would be short-circuited, and the arrival of the Beatles would come to symbolize the dawn of pop music as a social force unable to be dismissed. Especially when contrasted with the Beatles (who along with Elvis personified an adolescent hysteria akin to, but quite distinct from, the one that "Frankie" had begun in the early 1940s), a youthful Sinatra can only emphasize an atmosphere lacking the social unrest and experimentation associated with the Liverpool group in the mid- to late-1960s. The song's conclusion, with its melancholic farewell, thus can only push Frank even further into a distant, almost mythical, past—a golden age of eternal morning.

Sinatra did not freeze in 1963 either, however, and represents for the mid-80s British musicians yet another complication of time's passage. Clearly, the Dream Academy's primary audience would, in general, be unfamiliar with Sinatra's earlier incarnations as big band singer, object of bobby-soxer affection, and swinger. Instead, the singer's older, conservative, and tuxedoed image would spring first to mind, only to need retrofitting by the song's clear designation of an earlier Sinatra incarnation. Confronted with the necessary redefinition and/or recategorization that comes with the recognition of a hitherto unknown past of an icon, the audience now must face its own disorientation—a clear example of the complexities inherent in interpreting the past. Similar in effect to the song's opening images and similarly elusive, the past continues to distance itself from the present even as people fight to cling to some safe (and nostalgic) understanding of it. The song thus engages the listener in asking how present the past really is. The past, like the man on the train, never bids farewell entirely. And like those watching from the platform, as time moves on, no one is ever left unchanged.

"September Skies," more than any of the other songs discussed in this chapter,[20] aims at fully evoking the Sinatra sound and image with not only a theme and lyrics that recall some of his recordings but also through the musical arrangements and crooning style of singer/songwriter Brian Setzer. The song, a plaintive meditation on love, loss, and the passage of time invokes Sinatra early in the first verse and never really allows the listener to forget him. Indeed, it offers up Sinatra's music as much as a symbol of time's passage as the coming of autumn itself. The song metaphorically represents a man's reflections on his past. With the summer now over, as the singer comes to recognize his folly in thinking that youthful love could last forever, he sits isolated under the autumnal heavens of the title with (so listeners only can imagine) Sina-tra's singing in the background.

The theme and images of the song, of course, cannot but recall Sina-tra's recordings of "September Song," "September of My Years," "All Alone," and even "Summer Wind." Unlike the vintage songs "There's a Rainbow 'Round My Shoulder," "Route 66," and "A Nightingale Sang in Berkeley Square," which also appear on Setzer's 1994 album, however, "September Skies" (along with the album's opening track, "Lady Luck") avoids direct comparison with the past because, while in-voking the Sinatra muse, it is a new composition.[21] Sinatra conse-quently serves Setzer as an original theme upon which he plays his own variation. While perhaps analogous to some vintage Sinatra recordings, his composition and performance are meant to be viewed neither as simple homage nor through the lens of ironic distance but as a contem-porary, albeit "retro," setting for a timeless theme.[22]

Perhaps not surprisingly, it is two female songwriters who dissect and critique Sinatra's place as an icon whose swinging lifestyle (rather than music) is envied by so many men. But while Rickie Lee Jones's haunt-ing "Pirates (So Long Lonely Avenue)" highlights the piquancy of the "sad-eyed sinatras" of her past, Benett in her "Frank Sinatra" focuses upon the folly of these would-be Franks.

"Pirates (So Long Lonely Avenue)," the title track to Rickie Lee Jones's 1981 album, bids farewell to the "buddy boys" and "sad-eyed sinatras" with whom she had grown up. Jones, who often evokes the hard-edged and (alternately) desperate and buoyant life of urban youth, recalls life on "Lonely Avenue" (populated as it is with every-one, especially Joey, with whom she used to "ride in the middle . . . just trying to have some fun"). No longer able to "hold on to his rainbow sleeves," as she did when they would ride in his '57 Lincoln, she parts hoping that, perhaps, he also might escape. She never will forget him and, indeed, promises that in some future place—somewhere away from here—she will "see [him] there / Wait and see." Nevertheless, throughout the song (and, in fact, throughout the entire album), there is, amidst the whimsy of memory, a palpably keen sense of regret that boys like Joey never will "get the chance to make it" or to "just reach right out and take it." He, like all the other "sad-eyed sinatras," is doomed to remain on "Lonely Avenue," trapped by youthful fancy, un-able to translate the pirate life of a big man on campus into an adult voy-age through the "cold globe around the sea." Nowhere to go, they remain in their little world.

A similarly themed treatment, albeit with an entirely different tone, is Benett's "Frank Sinatra." From her 1996 disc, *So You're Not Coming Over*, the satiric song mentions Sinatra directly only in the title. Instead, by a clever allusion to his 1958 recording of Irving Berlin's "Cheek to Cheek" from *Come Dance with Me*, the singer/songwriter demonstrates how most, if not all, guys simply cannot (and perhaps should not even try to) live up to Frank's supposedly rakish lifestyle of women, Jack Daniels, and music. The action of the song takes place at a club, bar, or party and has the "finest guy" she's ever seen "sipping scotch on the rocks" poised to hit on her. Absent of all the romance that surrounds the Sinatra of the Capitol years, however, this man only can ape the swagger he must imagine Frank possesses:

> First cheek to cheek
> He'd swish it around
> He drank that scotch
> Without a frown.

Even as he puts "his hand right on her hip," however, he continues to drink—only to pass out drunk and immediately "hit the floor." All attitude and no substance, even this "finest guy" utterly fails to capture the Sinatra he wants so desperately to emulate.

Along with the punning allusion and comic conclusion to her tale, Benett employs a variety of formal touches that make her point. The extensive repetition of the lyrics (each line is repeated immediately and then each verse, upon completion, is sung again in its entirety) together with the very stripped down, but driving, arrangement of guitars, bass, and percussion, for example, only further emphasizes the utter shallowness of the interaction. The guy, consequently, appears neither clever nor subtle and merits neither pity nor reflection. As the song itself dismissively states, "That's all there is, there is no more."

For both Rickie Lee Jones and Benett, therefore, the "Sinatra" image remains a goal that boys cannot reach and true men would never attempt. By only aiming at imitation (and only a pale imitation, at that, as suggested by both writers' placing the singer's name in lower case), these boys fail to act authentically and, consequently, fail to mature. In Jones's song, this failure to grow takes on an almost tragic cast as it mourns all the Joeys who, perhaps in other circumstances, might have amounted to something. Benett's condemnation of the males of the mid-1990s, however, paints a far harsher picture of boys who are self-absorbed and impotent: too deluded to know how asinine they are acting and too insubstantial to hold even their liquor.

A male view of such macho posturing (joined, as it is, with a healthy dose of self-loathing) is in evidence on Helmet's 1992 heavy metal song "Sinatra." In it, songwriter Page Hamilton portrays being stuck driving around town with a young lady unable to satisfy his lust without what he deems unnecessary complication and distraction. Concerned with issues of commitment and birth control, the woman in the song demands more than the boy is either able or willing to give; even simple conversation and a modicum of sincerity seem beyond him. Indeed, he becomes disgusted with the situation and himself. His low self-esteem, however, does not prevent him from selfishly seeking satisfaction and, in the end, consummating the act (such as it is) with her.

His clear sense of entitlement to an uncomplicated encounter, as well as the probably subconscious recognition that he does not deserve even what little he gets, is underscored by his allusion to the now famous slogan " It's Frank's world, we just live in it." In other words, there ought to be a certain acceptance of what men should be allowed. His immediate problem is that this girl fails to comprehend her appropriate place and function in that world. He, according to his understanding of the concept, simply should not have to work as hard as she is making him. And, not surprisingly, their essentially anonymous act proves disappointing, alienating, and even cost-ineffective.

What the boy seems to accept as a given, what he takes for his birth right, of course, is nothing but the delusion he shares with all the "sad-eyed sinatras" found in the songs of Rickie Lee Jones and Benett. The sadness in their eyes is finally only a bitter mix of melodrama and frustration, the harsh results of the concurrence of conquest and farce.[23]

Elvis Costello tackles a similar theme in "The Deportees Club" from his 1984 album with the Attractions, *Goodbye Cruel World*. But while Helmet focuses exclusively on the isolation of the individual male, the Irish singer/songwriter employs Sinatra as a symbol for an estrangement inherent in American culture. Set in an exotically-named night spot, the song spins a dense lyrical web of alienation, tawdry associations, and failed connections. From its anonymous flirtations to its chorus of seven different types of alcohol from around the world, the song recreates an atmosphere too frenzied to foster real relationships. Instead, by evening's end, the man who had arrived with money is left without even his fare home. Thus ensured of loneliness, he can only beseech heaven for Sinatra's storied but clandestine past, a prayer he knows will never come true. Consequently, the speaker must remain forever on the margins of American society, a deportee of the title, since in the United States all that matters is one's sexual conquests. Unable to relate to anyone, the speaker feels he has failed to abide by the one truly American code. Consequently, as would one without passport, visa, or green card, the speaker knows what to expect: unceremonious and anonymous removal. Sent packing, he forever must remain apart and alone, victim of what one critic terms "a bewildering rootlessness" (Gouldstone 129).[24]

Costello's lyric, unlike Helmet's, refuses to remain on the merely personal level; his immigration and naturalization conceit transforms Sinatra's romantic reputation (and the twisted values upon which it rests) into a symbol of American hubris and hypocrisy. Sinatra's clandestine history, after all, despite what the speaker suggests, was hardly unfamiliar. Stories of the women, the feuds, the underworld connections continued for so long that they all became, like his music and his movies, part of a worldwide collective memory. True or not, they all contributed to the mythic Sinatra—the entertainer, the personality, and the American. Generous and unforgiving, remarkably talented and capable of supreme pettiness, friend of presidents and acquaintance of mobsters, Sinatra came to embody the nation . . . the good and the bad, and Costello forces the listener to confront that.

Nor can it be overlooked that Costello's juxtaposition of heaven and the tabloid reality of Sinatra's past foregrounds the clear incongruity of two of the most common images of Americans: an apparently devout churchgoing nation[25] and, at best, an amoral commercial juggernaut. Also suggesting a larger-scale critique of American values is the title of the song that, considering Costello's vast interest in and knowledge of a variety of musical idioms (Clayton-Lea 6–7), most probably alludes to Woody Guthrie's "Deportees (Plane Wreck at Los Gatos)," in which the folk singer critiques the dehumanizing nature of American culture by portraying the total indifference of the American public to the tragic deaths of a planeload of immigrant workers in 1947.

Given this view of America, being deported from the culture should be seen to have its advantages. Unfortunately, America's grasp extends so far and wide—as the international varieties of alcohol in the chorus attest—that there seems no viable alternative to it. Being outside of American culture, if that even is the correct term, is apparently to be nowhere.

An even more harshly critical view of America is offered in "The Sound of North America" by the British band, The Beautiful South.[26] From their 1996 album *Blue Is the Colour*, the song reinterprets American entertainment icons like Elvis Presley, Muhammed Ali, Greta Garbo, and Frank Sinatra in the harsh light of race and class. Never what it purports itself to be, America hides its true essence as a pompous, greedy, hypocritical, and racist society that turns its back on those who need the most help.[27] The chorus of the song, in fact, addresses a different facet of American life each time it is sung: a laissez-faire economy that rests upon the back of its poor (5–6), a Christian nation that regularly acts contrary to its professed beliefs (15–16), and a white culture—here symbolized by Sinatra—that plunders the artistic modes of its minorities and celebrates them as its own creations (25–26).[28] In short, the entire culture of America, such as it is, rests upon the impoverished and enslaved.

The indictment is so pointed that its mention of Sinatra's debt to swinging African Americans takes on ominous overtones. While probably echoing Allen Ginsberg's insightful phrase "Frank Sinatra with negro voice" in "Bayonne Turnpike to Tuscarora" from *The Fall of America* (468), the song's reference to Sinatra clearly aims to evoke both the black singers, like Louis Armstrong and Billie Holiday, to whom Sinatra's art owes so much (Pleasants 107, 190), and the lengthy roster of lynching victims throughout nineteenth- and twentieth-century American history.[29] Sinatra thus offers simply one more (very famous) face of racism, of the co-opting by the dominant culture of the lives and the art forms of the marginalized.[30]

The dreams that America offers its citizens and the world and then, too often, reneges on are also central to mentions of Sinatra in both Prefab Sprout's 1988 "Hey Manhattan!" and the Pogues' 1987 "Fairy Tale of New York." "Hey Manhattan!," taken from the album *From Langley Park to Memphis* (itself an extended meditation on the meaning of America), ponders the American:

> myths we can't undo they lie in wait for you
> we live them till they're true.

Since every place from the Brooklyn Bridge to the Carlyle Hotel possesses some fabled association, just spending time in New York City cannot help but make one feel that:

> the world's on my side . . . [with]
> A billion souls all dying to know me.

"Strolling Fifth Avenue" is exhilarating, after all, because "Sinatra's been here too," and the ensuing "star struck" giddiness even makes one warble "doobie doo . . . doobie doo."

Unfortunately, being "loaded with promise/and knee deep in grace" changes, after reference to JFK's assassination ("Yeah some things are slow to fade"), into being "knee deep in [a] fate [that] . . . litters the whole damn place." "Star struck" subsequently becomes "bad luck," "strolling Fifth Avenue" turns to "scrounging," and "the poor" replace "Sinatra." The dream that America offered at the opening of the song is thus no longer so welcoming, and the promise of actualizing its myths now sounds more like a threat. The nightmarish side of American prosperity reveals itself and, by song's end, sours everything—even the scatting of "Strangers in the Night":

> But what are [the poor] to do? These myths belong to you
> We live them till they're true,
> Manhattan doobie doo.

With the American dream deflated, the vacuity of the response to poverty, "doobie doo . . . doobie doo," thus becomes utterly apparent.

The intimate association of Frank Sinatra, New York, and America is at the heart of the Pogues' song, as well.[31] A fractured fairy tale of an Irish couple who, while traveling in New York, split on a Christmas Eve memorable only for its name-calling and doing time in jail for public drunkenness, the song offers Sinatra's music as an integral part of the promise of a dreamlike American holiday. This trip of a lifetime, financed by his having a good day at the racetrack, is a chance to make their dreams a reality. New York, after all, is a place meant for the young like them, where the streets are lined with gold and the future is open to whatever they desire. He promises her a night she will never forget, a time that will be festive indeed. All is well in America, or so it seems.

The juxtaposition, within the festivities, of Sinatra's music and a chorus of drunks, however, immediately and succinctly captures both the dichotomous nature of the city (its glamour and poverty) and the ease with which the less desirable elements can be ignored in the face of the romance that New York offers. New York, admittedly, while filled with the promise of large automobiles and riches, is not always so hospitable. As the lyrics make clear, the city's harsh elements and hectic pace can make it a brutal place to live; as a result, America only tolerates the strong.

The lovers, due to their infatuation with each other and their fascination with the new surroundings, are oblivious to their own frailties—an oversight a night in the city quickly corrects. Early in the evening, for example, they are complimentary and tender, but quickly they turn insulting and cruel. By the time they are trading the worst insults, the blackly comic nature of this journey to the New World is revealed. In the last verse, when he fecklessly boasts of his own potential[32]—a claim she bluntly dismisses—it is clear that New York is but America writ small. For New York manifests the same cruel realities of American success and failure: the celebrity that accompanies prosperity and the anonymity that follows the destitute (and vice versa).

Perhaps not surprisingly, three of these last four songs were written and performed by groups from the British Isles during the U.S. presidency of Ronald Reagan, with "Reaganomics" and (by association) the economic and social policies of conservative British Prime Minister Margaret Thatcher, as the ultimate targets of the critiques.[33] (Elvis Costello, for example, levels an ad hominem attack against Reagan in another song from *Goodbye Cruel World*, "Peace in Our Time," when he dismisses the commander in chief as a brainless space cadet.[34]) Frank Sinatra, as the most visible friend of the Reagans and organizer of Reagan's 1981 inaugural gala, thus metamorphoses in the songs into the musical voice of the right wing political agenda. And, as that voice, in the eyes of its critics, he becomes symbolic of all the excesses and liable for all the injustices resulting from those policies. In short, Frank Sinatra, the pop singer, takes on a new title: enemy of the people.

From the beginning of his career, Sinatra presented songwriters with a remarkably substantial canvas upon which they could depict their diverse thoughts, desires, and concerns. From the personal to the political, from the carnal to the musical, from "high priest of *eros*" to the personification of 1980s greed, these incarnations of Sinatra spoke to each ensuing generation. While never exactly their father's Sinatra, each new manifestation shared at least one characteristic with its predecessors: the realization that few, if any, contemporary public figures other than Sinatra could bear the weight of meaning so much to so many. For so many musicians, to paraphrase and qualify Pete Hamill, *only* Sinatra mattered.

NOTES

1. Even earlier, in December 1944, while recording with Stan Kenton and his orchestra, Anita O'Day interpolated Sinatra's name into the lyrics of Hal Dickinson's "Tabby the Cat."

2. The close affinity of the two singers was underscored at the time by such jokes as Bob Hope's humorous introduction of Sinatra on his February 13, 1946, V-Disc recording of "The Song is You": "When Bing Crosby was fourteen he had his adenoids removed, and here's one of them now: Frankie Sinatra."

3. Further evidence of the dominance of Sinatra and Crosby can be found in the Warner Brothers' cartoon, "Swooner Crooner," featuring Porky Pig as the manager of "Flockheed Eggcraft," a chicken ranch. In the animated short, which received an Oscar nomination in 1944, Porky is faced with the predicament of chickens which have stopped producing because they have been distracted so completely by an emaciated rooster named Frankie. After interviewing several roosters (including fowl versions of Vaughn Monroe, Jimmy Durante, and Cab Calloway) to make his hens productive again, the porcine manager turns to one named Bing, the only one up to the task. The ensuing competition between the two crooning roosters is so hard-fought (and, as a result, productive) that, by the end, even Porky is laying scores of eggs! No one, it seems, can deliver such surefire commercial response better than Bing and Frank, and no one is immune.

4. The identical point is made in a very different song, Slim Gaillard's encyclopedic "Jumpin' at the Record Shop," also from 1945. Despite containing an impressive roster of contemporary recording artists, only Bing and Frank are clearly designated as the first among equals. Another encyclopedic song from 1945, "I'd Rather Be with You," a Doris Day/Johnny Parker duet with Les Brown's big band, also includes Sinatra (rhymed with Sumatra!) along with an extensive list of Hollywood names including Greer Garson, Joan Blondell, Laurel and Hardy, and Clark Gable.

5. Travis later would have another connection to Sinatra when the country singer performed "Re-enlistment Blues" in the film *From Here to Eternity*.

6. Bruce Bliven's November 6, 1944, piece for *The New Republic*, "The Voice and the Kids," offers an excellent example of this type of article. In it, Bliven essentially argues that Frank Sinatra, a pleasant enough singer, means so much to the bobby-soxers because American culture has failed to give them anything else of substance to which to cling.

7. See appendix II.

8. One of the few examples is Matt Monro's 1964 recording of "It's a Breeze," which sets up Sinatra's well-known ring-a-ding-ding lifestyle as paradigmatic of the good life. This song, however (as was the Henry Mancini title song for the 1961 MGM film *Bachelor in Paradise*), clearly was directed toward adult listeners and therefore champions the pre-rock music style favored by that demographic. Matt Monro, of course, who came to be known as "the British Sinatra," got his big break when he served as an ersatz Sinatra singing "You Keep Me Swingin'" on Peter Sellers's 1959 comedy album, *Songs for Swingin' Sellers*.

9. As a case in point, attempting to escape her father's imposing musical shadow, Natalie Cole during the mid-1970s distanced herself as much and as often as possible from Nat King Cole's musical legacy. In early interviews, she not infrequently bristled at the notion of being considered "Nat Cole's daughter." As she aged, however, she not only stopped rejecting that associa-

tion, she came to embrace it fully even by recording duets with the deceased singer.

In contrast, Frank Sinatra, Jr. never attempted to put his father or his music at even arm's length and consequently has remained almost entirely—and unfairly—in his shadow ever since. Admittedly, as his sister, Tina, suggests in her 2000 book, *My Father's Daughter* (92), he did not help himself by going against the tide of rock music and so consistently and blatantly associating himself with his father's music by working with the Pied Pipers and Nelson Riddle or titling his 1972 album *His Way*. Nevertheless, even after decades of establishing for himself a reputation of fine musicianship, he continues to suffer severely from being "Junior." How else could one explain, a full year-and-a-half after his father's death, why his billing as "Sinatra" for a November 1999 concert could be termed "misleading" by the *Hartford Courant* (11/18/99)? Did anyone really think that his father might appear? (Unlike her brother, and even though she recorded several duets with her father while he was alive, Nancy Sinatra avoided the same fate by first establishing herself in her own musical idiom in 1966 with the number one hit "These Boots Were Made for Walking.")

10. Surprisingly, unlike younger musicians who began to examine the meaning of Sinatra, Paul Anka, the lyricist of such Sinatra songs as "My Way" and "Let Me Try Again," only offers his listeners a Sinatra who still commands attention in the title track of his 1979 album, *Headlines*. The song, a satire on the tide of information that floods the average American, offers Frank as just one of many examples of the stories the press pursues and publishes. Sinatra, Muhammed Ali, and Jackie Kennedy Onassis, along with more ephemeral figures as "First Brother" Billy Carter, are part of the litany of topics that, in the end, only overwhelm the public: judicial decisions, legislative action, nuclear energy, geopolitical maneuvering, and, naturally, celebrity news. In the Anka/Sammy Cahn lyric, however, Sinatra's presence signifies little more than that Sinatra still merited headline status, that even at sixty-four he was still newsworthy. Oddly enough, his newsworthiness ("Sinatra's still swinging / that don't mean he's singing") seems more of a raucous sexual—as opposed to a musical—nature, which is intriguing considering that, by 1979, he had been married to Barbara Marx for nearly three years. Perhaps more interesting, however, is that, while alluding more appropriately to the way Sinatra probably behaved twenty years earlier, the lyric completely neglects Sinatra's return to recording in July of that year for his monumental three-record set, *Trilogy*, his first studio album in more than five years. So much for the timeliness of these headlines!

11. Manilow's title perhaps alludes to "Here's to the Band," Sinatra's 1983 salute to all the musicians with whom he had performed throughout his career. The song, which had been composed as a salute to the American Federation of Musicians (Friedwald, *The Song Is You* 486), was in turn revised by Ray Anthony into a salute to Frank, "Here's to Sinatra."

12. This calls to mind another Irishman, U2's lead singer, Bono, whose introduction of Sinatra on the Grammy Awards in 1996 focused much of its praise on the singer's toughness and survival skills.

13. On the same album, Morrison pays another, less obvious, compliment to Sinatra by recording "Green" (a Joe Raposo song about nonconformity originally written for the Jim Henson character "Kermit the Frog" of *Sesame Street* fame), which Sinatra himself had chosen to include on his 1968 album, *My Way*. It surely must have turned at least as many heads among Morrison's audience as it had among Sinatra's.

14. This recalls a song about the perils of success that Randy Newman had written with hopes that Frank Sinatra might record it, "Lonely at the Top" (Newman 51).

15. Only Smash Mouth, in its 1997 "Padrino," taps exclusively into the long tradition of Sinatra's alleged mob ties by using "to sing" as slang for "to testify."

16. Although not specifically invoked, the spirit of Sinatra also hangs over Veitch's "Pledging Allegiance," the opening track of the album. In it, the American dream—as epitomized by show business and quick lucrative trips to Vegas—clearly encourages the listener to think of Sinatra (as well as other musical icons such as Hank Williams and Elvis Presley). This dimension of the song is made even clearer when interpreted in light of subsequent songs such as "Frank Sinatra," "Las Vegas Sand," and "Bottom of the Bottle."

17. Mannix, in their 1999 song "Sinatra's Dead," plays a similar trick with its title. While the listener might expect the song to be a rallying cry for a new musical order, the song is really a nicely elegiac instrumental expressing a sincere sense of loss.

18. For the same unreleased *Adult Child* album from 1977, Brian Wilson composed "Still I Dreamed of It" with Sinatra in mind, although never approached him to record it.

19. Here, lyricist John McCrea most probably is alluding to the March 24, 1957, recording of the song released on the Capitol album *No One Cares*. Sinatra made two other studio recordings of the song: on December 3, 1944, at Columbia Records and on May 17, 1984, for his *L.A. Is My Lady* released on Quincy Jones's Qwest label, neither of which matches the Capitol version in Sinatra's vocal interpretation.

20. The one exception would have to be "It's a Breeze" which, taking full advantage of Matt Monro's status as "The British Sinatra," clearly aims at approximating, as closely as possible, the ring-a-ding-ding feel of the real Sinatra.

21. Sinatra did record "A Nightingale Sang in Berkeley Square" for his *Great Songs from Great Britain* album, but it certainly never became closely associated with him the way so many other songs did, such as "September of My Years," "Summer Wind," and "Luck Be a Lady." And while some have speculated that it is Sinatra singing on a recently surfaced recording of

"Nightingale," the late-1930s disk would have been unknown to Setzer in 1994.

22. Throughout his career, Setzer has shown this same interest in contemporizing the sound of earlier music. As leader of the Stray Cats, for example, his focus was "rockabilly" and, with his eponymous orchestra, it is now "big band" music.

23. The cover of Connie Dungs's 1998 ironically named album, *Songs for Swinging Nice Guys*, pithily highlights the distance between Sinatra and the rest of mortal men, with its picture of a man who has hanged himself (which the band very well may have borrowed from a similar sight gag that Peter Sellers had used for the cover of his 1959 *Songs for Swingin' Sellers*).

24. In this spirit, Irish singer Christy Moore included the song on his 1989 album, *Voyager* (Clayton-Lea 224).

25. The United States regularly appears at or very near the top of surveys on church attendance and its citizens' description of themselves as "religious."

26. The band's interest in Sinatra is apparent also on "Old Red Eyes Is Back," the opening track of their 1992 album, *0898*.

27. Their melancholic remake of the swinging Bobby Darin hit "Artificial Flowers," the story of an orphan girl who freezes to death alone in a tenement house, makes a similar point.

28. Throughout the twentieth century, such charges have been leveled against white artists as different as George Gershwin and Paul Simon.

29. The reference to the shuffling about of the homeless in an earlier chorus also cannot help but suggest the stereotyping of black figures in American popular culture, as heard on such shows as *Amos 'n' Andy*, which happened to be one of Sinatra's favorite radio programs and on which he appeared in 1954. In fact, Freeman Gosden, who played George "Kingfish" Stevens on the program, was so close to Sinatra that he was the singer's best man when he married Barbara in 1976 (Tollin 42).

30. Rhythm-and-blues singer Johnnie Taylor offers a counterpoint to this view in his 1984 "That's America," which posits, at least musically speaking, a racially diverse nation made up of Nat Cole, Frank Sinatra, and Stevie Wonder. The song also recalls Sinatra's 1945 song about racial and religious tolerance, "The House I Live In (What Is America to Me)."

31. The association of the man and the city is a common one and, given the popularity of his 1979 recording of Kander and Ebb's "New York, New York" (not to mention Green and Comden's "New York, New York" from 1949's *On the Town*), completely understandable. See also chapter 10.

32. This line from the lyric faintly echoes the famous line from *On the Waterfront*, which would be quite appropriate since Sinatra himself actively sought the role of Terry Molloy in the 1955 film but lost it to Marlon Brando—the very actor who won another role Sinatra had wanted: Sky Masterson in the film version of *Guys and Dolls* (Nancy Sinatra 119).

33. Consider the opening of Irish singer Sinead O'Connor's 1990 "Black Boys on Mopeds," in which she equates the actions of Margaret Thatcher's government with the Chinese communist crackdown at Tiananmen Square.

34. To tie the songs more closely together thematically, "Peace in Our Time," the concluding song of the album, also revisits the international nightclub metaphor introduced in "Deportees Club."

CHAPTER 7

The Universal Tongue:
Language and Image
in Raul Nuñez's *Sinatra*

Frank Sinatra in numerous ways has come to represent the United States, both positively and negatively, for many people worldwide. On account of this intimate association with things American, Sinatra's very visible presence on the international cultural landscape should come as no surprise.[1] Upon his death, countries ranging from the Republique Federale Islamique des Cormores and Somalia to Türkmenistan and Zaire issued commemorative stamps. In 1999, Israeli filmmaker Nadav Levitan wrote and directed the drama *Frank Sinatra Is Dead*. Stories of how Japanese schools have used Sinatra's records as a model of English pronunciation also have long been reported. In fact, this "Sinatra approach" to second language acquisition has reached our own shores, as well. In May 1999, the "About NY" column in the *New York Times* ran a story of the academic success of a young Ecuadoran immigrant whose deli boss/English instructor recommended that the then-seventeen-year-old listen to Frank Sinatra records to improve his English.[2] Sinatra, thus, not only stands out as one who "speaks American" but, at the same time, somehow manages to connect with those who do not have English.

This powerful connection is quite evident, for example, when watching tapes of Sinatra's 1962 concerts in Japan. On the video, it becomes clear that the audience—while not comprehending much, if anything, of the meaning of the lyrics Sinatra sings—is nevertheless caught up in the music and, especially, his performance. The Sinatra persona thus has a hold on his audience that is quite distinct from his lyrical content—be they the words of a Porter, Cahn, Gershwin, or Kern.

It is this same attraction of the Sinatra persona that Raul Nuñez dissects in his 1984 Spanish novella, *Sinatra*, translated into English by Ed Emery as *The Lonely Hearts Club*. His story, set in a sleazy Barcelona hotel, of the romantic travails of a night porter who bears a remarkable resemblance to Frank Sinatra never allows its readers to forget that the American icon, and all that his name and multiplicity of images imply, has a universal significance. Not to be relegated simply to an American scene, Sinatra's aura both haunts and offers hope to the often-tortured souls who populate the novella.[3]

Sinatra tells the story of the forty-year-old Antonio who, due to his resemblance to the famous singer, more commonly is known as "Frankie." As the novella begins, the reader learns that the previous year Frankie had been abandoned by his wife for a black man. His self-dissolution ensues. Drinking heavily and abandoning his job as a successful door-to-door salesman, he winds up the "night porter" at a "cheap hotel in Calle Hospital" (Nuñez 10). In an attempt to right himself, at least romantically, Frankie enrolls in a mail-order lonely hearts club through which he receives responses from an increasingly bizarre roster of correspondents: a widow, a transsexual, an ex-con, a midget poet, and a homicidal religious zealot. Together with the sibling hotel owners, a sex-crazed fellow porter, a prostitute, and a runaway addict who thinks she is the mother of Frankie's child, Antonio's bachelor existence is rarely solitary.

Clearly, Nuñez's darkly comic scenario seems as far away from Sinatra's public (and personal) life as it possibly could be. Nevertheless, the singer's presence pervades the novella. Various female characters, for example, mention Antonio's resemblance to Sinatra.[4] It is the characteristic that first drew his ex-wife to him (10). It is also what first attracts both Hortensia Garcia, the widow (13), and Begonia Montana, the midget poet (53). Senorita Clementina, sister of the recently deceased owner of the hotel, also alludes to it with the far-fetched idea that Hollywood might want to hire him as a Sinatra double (91).

Over the course of the novella, Antonio himself also begins to accept, and draw strength from, his close affinity with Sinatra. He signs his letter to the widow with "Frank Sinatra" (Nuñez 17), for instance. Another example is at the bar when he first notices Natalia, the cross-eyed girl with the doll she comes to think is Antonio's child. At first, he is tense and tongue-tied. When she asks for a cigarette, however, something or someone else takes over: " 'Help yourself,' he said. His words came out smooth as honey. As if it hadn't been him speaking, but the real Sinatra. She smiled" (21). At this point, the unconscious power he draws from Sinatra is short-lived and even a bit delusional since he immediately must correct his reference to himself as "Frankie" (23).

Nevertheless, his resemblance to the singer remains an inspiration to him, for, as time goes on, he summons the courage to read yet another club response by first comparing his mirrored reflection to a magazine photo of Sinatra in Las Vegas (Nuñez 52–53). And even later—immediately following the murder of the prostitute, Isabel, by her pimp (120–121)—face to face with his reflection, he carries on a full conversation with Sinatra concerning the options the remaining women in his life offer (125–126).

That Antonio has internalized Sinatra to some degree also is suggested further by the passing allusions to Sinatra films and recordings both when he opens a letter with the exhortation "OK, chum, Anchors away!" (31)[5] as well as his letter to Begonia Montana, in which he complains to her that, while other club members are "driving me crazy . . . you can count on me" (109).[6] Inspiration, escape, and alter ego, Sinatra challenges Antonio to continue to function in a crazy world turned ugly—but, of course, that is before the virgin-midget-poet vomits on him in mid-embrace (141) and Brother Blanco Sol, believing him to be "the Wicked One," tries to execute him (147).

Clearly, one of the things that Sinatra offers the novelist is the classic pop singer's distinct difference from the pop music scene of the early 1980s. The classic pop standards Sinatra sings, and the romantically sophisticated culture often associated with them, stand in stark contrast to the contemporary music that infuses much of the action. For instance, when the eighty-three-year-old hotel owner, Señor Flores, better known to his employees as "the Lizard," forces Antonio to take him to a discotheque to meet women, the music playing at the club seems only to accentuate the loneliness of the characters: "The loudspeakers were blaring out wild rock and roll. Everybody was dancing or moving. Facing each other. Not touching each other. Not looking at each other. Not laughing either . . . Everyone seemed to be dancing alone" (Nuñez 61). The very dance music that should bring people together (which is, after all, the need that draws the Lizard there to begin

with) only encourages them to be solitary, self-contained, and discon-
nected from all those around them. In fact, this is the very atmosphere
that Elvis Costello conjures up in his song of the same year, "The Deportees Club," discussed in chapter 6. For even when the Lizard spots
the "carefree" and "unreal" woman "I knew that I'd find," her appeal is
utterly anonymous (61): An enormous mass of golden hair. A waterfall
of locks . . . They moved on the girl's shoulders like a magic spider, with
a life of its own, and a sweet and mysterious smell" (61–62). Helplessly
attracted to the smell and the hair, the Lizard approaches her, plunges
his face in "the entrails of that golden tarantula," and dies (62).

The incredible allure of the raw power of rock music is surely at issue here. Its appeal is undeniable, but as potent and sensual as the music might be, the isolation and loneliness of the rock culture cannot be
denied either. While perhaps momentarily cheerful, Señor Flores cannot be considered a happy man at his death since he dies a "heart-bro-
ken ghost" (62) never even having seen the woman's face. A nameless
vision close enough to touch but too remote to know is apparently the
best the rock world has to offer, and that clearly should not be
enough.

The emptiness of contemporary rock and roll is again alluded to in
the "Sid Vicious Is Dead" T-shirt worn by Contreras, a local sibyl to
whom Antonio's barber directs him for the answers to his questions.
While "mad as a hatter," according to Camacho, Contreras just "might
give [Antonio] an idea" of what he should do (Nuñez 94). And, in fact,
after the prophet chastises Antonio at forty years of age for still taking
women seriously at all (96), he directs Antonio to avoid Hortensia,
Natalia, and even Isabel—the prostitute with whom Antonio had spent
a remarkable night free-of-charge (81)—to pursue Begonia Montana.
As Contreras says: "[Midgets are] no trouble, they don't bug you. They
don't crowd your space. Everybody passes over them, but it doesn't
worry them. They look at life from below, and have a very different take
on it . . . They have more worldly wisdom. They're more real than other
women" (96). Contreras, as his name implies, is offering an alternative
view and celebrates the nontraditional. While perhaps not altogether
correct in his assessment of the situation (Antonio's rendezvous with
Montana ends in utter comic horror), he is also far from wrong. Antonio's circumstances certainly merit thinking "outside of the box," and
Contreras's odd take on the night porter's options is appropriately
novel. Logic is rarely the strong suit of seers; they tend to divine the
truth through other means.

And that is how his T-shirt with the Sid Vicious headline enters the equation. The death of the bass player of that archetypal punk band, the Sex Pistols, on February 2, 1979, intimates much about the longevity and musical accomplishments of Sinatra. For The Sex Pistols' celebrated version of "My Way" crystallizes the extremism of punk rock as the ultimate rejection of the status quo. As Robert Pattison writes in *The Triumph of Vulgarity*, it was Vicious's very "lack of talent" that "made him a star in the rock pantheon" (Pattison 136). His having "played no instrument before joining the Sex Pistols in 1977," allowed him to be: "the youthful Everyman suddenly transformed by the liberating pantheism in which all things are permitted and self-annihilation provides an avenue to self-realization. Sid was the ultimate creation of the modern Prometheus, a creature of electricity's democratic current. Poor monster!" (Pattison 136). Vicious, in short, was punk rock's reply to Sinatra, who in his own right was the democratic voice of several generations. Ironically, it was the young Vicious (and not Sinatra) who already was dead.

The reference to his death in 1979 (the very year that Sinatra would be reclaiming his status as pop's premier artist with *Trilogy*) suggests a critique of the emptiness of rock's rebellion in the late 1970s and early 1980s. For if rock is at its core "an idea . . . a denunciation of everything old, smug, and wistful" (Pattison x), then, according to Nuñez, it is an idea that has bankrupted itself. Having arrived at the point where musical talent was unnecessary (and the very lack of it seemingly a prerequisite!) to be a musical star, how could Sinatra—as musician and celebrity—serve as anything but an icon of quality and significance, an image of hope for the lonely and struggling. Having refused to self- destruct like the "poor monster" Vicious (who murdered his girlfriend and took his own life but three months later), Sinatra and his art continue on.[7]

Sinatra, however, despite the *Sgt. Pepper*-esque title given its English translation, is not primarily concerned with popular music, its societal role, or its decline. Everything about the novella suggests that it is concerned with the human need for love and the difficulties people face in finding it. That this Sinatra look-alike turns to a collection of photographs of other lonely people to find some connection suggests a central place for Sinatra in twentieth-century romance. The question is what his place and significance are, especially in a world as far from Frank's as Antonio's would seem to be.

One of the few times that Antonio seems to have the world on a string and lives a life even remotely approximating Sinatra's fabled existence is the evening he spends his enormous bingo purse, which he wins due to a lucky "idiot child" he rents to bring him luck (Nuñez 74–75), and tastes the high life with Isabel. His single night with her is "just like in the movies," and everything about it, from the "five-star hotel room" to the "wildest night of love-making ever," is remarkable (81–82). "For the first time in his life, he was king" (79), and, with a bravado quite unfamiliar to the reader, Antonio declares that this will be "the last time" they will ever "fuck about" with him (82). As Nuñez makes clear, however, as much as Antonio may want to be Sinatra—he even introduces himself as a singer to Isabel (76)—he is no Sinatra. The chapter, in fact, turns out to be a parody of Sinatra's Rat Pack life of gaming, booze, and broads—with bingo instead of dice, a prostitute instead of Jill St. John, etc.[8] This life as Sinatra, however, is seen to be but a chimera which begins to dissolve the next morning when Natalia returns addicted to smack (83–84) and continues when, even as he is falling in love with Isabel, he discovers that he has contracted syphilis from their encounter (105). Clearly, this scenario affirms that it cannot be Sinatra's more high-flying lifestyle that serves as his primary significance.

Instead, as Nuñez indicates when Clementina shows her collection of celebrity photographs to Antonio, Sinatra embodies a loneliness and a melancholy born of heartbreak that crosses lines of class and nationality. Antonio thinks that her album, filled with photos of "platinum blondes" and "famous actors," is utterly "different" from the "club's brochure, with its little photographs of each member" (131). How could anyone compare the two? But as she turns to her photo of Sinatra, readers cannot help but recognize the equivalence of the two albums. As Nuñez writes: "It was a picture of one of [Sinatra's] many weddings. His wife was small and pretty, with a face that was a bit bony and with blonde hair that had been cut too short. She looked about thirty years younger than her husband . . . Both of them were smiling. They looked happy" (131). The obvious mismatch of Sinatra and Mia Farrow powerfully argues the difficulties inherent in finding true love. For even if Sinatra himself confessed to daughter Nancy at the time: "I don't know maybe we'll only have a couple of years . . . But we have to try" (Nancy Sinatra 199), in retrospect their 1966 marriage must be considered nothing but a divorce waiting to happen. And Nuñez's emphasis on the actress' less than traditional beauty (her short stature, skinniness, and boyish hair), about which many of Frank's cronies joked endlessly at the time, reflects significantly on Antonio's trouble in finding the perfect woman to love . . . even as it perhaps foreshadows his date with the midget. If Frank Sinatra, a man who seemingly can have any woman he wants, must struggle to find that special someone, as this third of his "many marriages" would seem to indicate, then how can Antonio (or anyone) expect anything easier for himself?

The wedding photo thus accomplishes two things. First, on the level of plot, it encourages Antonio to try the club one final time: with Begonia.[9] Second, it perhaps suggests the theme of futility of Antonio's search, for the novella ends not with his finding love, but with his dying in the comforting and protective arms of Clementina. Her embrace has less to do with romantic love than it does with a maternal concern for the younger man and his need to be mothered. Pressed against her "warm breasts," Antonio slowly but steadily drifts away, unable to respond to her comforting words (Nuñez 151). In a sense, his being embraced by Clementina, whose name implies a mix of mercy and practicality, is his chance to shed his previous life and be reborn, to free himself from the weight of disappointment and death. He misses that chance, however, because his death intervenes.

It is Clementina, after all, who saves Antonio's life only moments before by disarming Brother Blanco Sol when he arrives at the hotel to kill "The Wicked One." Her simple act of removing her clothes in front of the madman reveals the would-be soldier of God as nothing more than a man who "for the first time in his life . . . has seen a woman with no clothes on" (Nuñez 149). Not one to overintellectualize, she zeroes in on a situation by recognizing the basic needs of the people she meets.[10] Just as Brother Blanco Sol, after seeing her naked, "wouldn't hurt a fly" (149), so Antonio first and foremost needs solace . . . and a shave (151). Of course, Antonio is similar to almost every other character, who seeks love but actually requires something even more basic—protection: Natalia from her addiction, Rosendo/Rosita from her abusive boyfriend, Hortensia from her own son, and Isabel from her pimp. While none of them finds that relief, Clementina is offering it to Antonio as he slips away at the conclusion of the novella, and they are her words on which it ends: "Take it easy, Frankie. Take it easy."

Clementina, who "understood everything" (Nuñez 150), thus exemplifies the mercy and forgiveness that Antonio/Frankie would seem to have merited for a persistence that held off his self-destruction for a considerable stretch of time (but obviously not long enough). The entire novella details his falling to pieces, and Brother Blanco Sol is "the last straw" (150), with which comes Antonio's slow, but final, surrender: "He shut his eyes and began to see a strange unaccustomed light approaching him, like the dawn" (151). He then answers " 'I will, I will' . . . as if from a distance" to Clementina's mention of a shave until finally he cannot respond at all (151). In her arms, he dies broken and lonely, if not alone. This image, almost a perverse "Pieta,"[11] suggests the meaning of Sinatra for Nuñez. Antonio dies for no reason. His death saves no one. His legacy is a sad but negligible one.

Sinatra's unique place in the world as artist and celebrity, on the contrary, is vital and life affirming. Just as Sinatra distinguishes himself from Sid Vicious who musically and personally destroyed himself, so Sinatra distinguishes himself from all who, having lost in life or love, accept defeat prematurely. Throughout his life, Sinatra had ample opportunity to surrender, but he never allowed himself to succumb. From Ava, Mitch Miller, and "red baiting" to Mia, Mafia allegations, and early retirement, Sinatra made a career of taking blows and somehow coming back. Even in the nourishing embrace of Clementina, however, Antonio no longer can summon the strength, will, or courage to carry on. Unlike his namesake, the hotel porter welcomes defeat. As Contreras's T-shirt might now read: "Frankie is dead! Long live Sinatra!"

NOTES

1. Consider also such diverse international details as an August 15, 1998, Sinatra tribute in Bad Laasphe, Germany, *Frank Sinatra und seine Zeit*; a club named "Sinatra" in Nerja, Spain; Brazilian Cauby Peixoto's 1992 compact disc, *Cauby Canta Sinatra*; a Spanish language version of Lew Irwin's *Sinatra, A Life Remembered* by Ana Alcaina, entitled *Sinatra Una Vida en Imágenes 1915–1998*; and the various life experiences of Sally de Mattia described in her 1999 essay, "A Personal Testimony and a View from Europe: The Multicultural Frank Sinatra." Tom Russell, in his 2001 song "When Sinatra Played Juarez," also explores Sinatra's cross-cultural significance and influence.

2. Pete Hamill, in *Why Sinatra Matters*, describes the phenomenon among Brooklynites (93–94), while the fictional Rosie Rosellini teaches her two sons a similar lesson in Michael Ventura's *The Death of Frank Sinatra*, a novel discussed further in chapter 10 (219).

3. In 1988, *Sinatra* was made into a film, written and directed by Spanish filmmaker Francisco Betriú and starring Alfredo Landa as "Antonio/Frankie" and Ana Obregón as "Isabel."

4. The ex-con Juan Cuevas Heredia only remarks that Antonio seems to have "a sympathetic face" (51).

5. In 1945, Sinatra co-starred with Gene Kelly in the MGM film *Anchors Aweigh*.

6. Sinatra recorded "You're Driving Me Crazy" for Reprise on May 11, 1966, and "Count on Me," with the other principals of *On the Town*, on March 24, 1949.

7. Playwright Bernard Kops examines Sinatra's own monstrous qualities in his *Playing Sinatra*, which is discussed in the next chapter.

8. A comparably comic, if only passing, play upon Sinatra's swinging image occurs in Tom Hazuka's *In the City of the Disappeared*, when Peace Corps volunteer Harry Bayliss patronizes the *Fuente de Soda Frank Sinatra*, the "Frank Sinatra Soda Fountain," in Santiago, Chile (133).

9. Significantly, the one Sinatra song that is mentioned by name in the novella is his 1973 recording of "Let Me Try Again," which Hortensia purchased especially for their dinner at her house (67).

10. While it is true that Juan Cuevas Heredia , the ex-con, hooks up with her for a while, then runs out with her forty thousand pesetas, the reader cannot help but sense that, while she enjoyed her time with him, she is not disappointed at his departure—even with the loss of money (145).

11. This association is not much of a stretch since, perversely, it is the Virgin Mary who Brother Blanco Sol says has ordered him to kill Antonio (106, 150).

CHAPTER 8

"There'll Be No Future Without Him": The Voice versus the Emerging Monster in *Playing Sinatra*

> People scoff. Psychiatrists dissect. But Sinatra people don't cause wars or commit acts of terrible violence. We adore him because he is unique. He is sweet and gentle. His face haunts all our lives, gives us hope, purpose. He lights up the world with his amazing but gentle power, his voice just ignites such love inside me. I love everyone, the world, everyone. I change things. Life has meaning. I change things.
>
> —Bernard Kops, *Playing Sinatra*

So says Sandra Lewis, as she and her brother, Norman, share their favorite pastime, "playing Sinatra," in British playwright Bernard Kops's 1991 drama of the same name (7).[1] In the two-act play, Kops depicts how the aging siblings attempt to grapple with the often-ugly realities of their world using the music and public image of Frank Sinatra as their primary defense. This chapter will examine the playwright's use of the entertainer's *oeuvre* as a means of characterizing and critiquing Norman and Sandra. Kops employs the paradoxical nature of the iconic Sinatra—alternately lover and loser, ally and bully, romantic and rake— both to underscore the siblings' fragile humanity and to critique their seemingly insurmountable fear of life.

Set in a stately but neglected Victorian in contemporary London, *Playing Sinatra* centers on a mentally unbalanced bookbinder and his sister who share their childhood home and survive on microwavable gourmet meals and all things Sinatra. As the audience is introduced to them, we see that, quite contrary to Sandra's declaration that "I change things," Norman and Sandra's life proceeds almost ritualistically (Kops 2). Norman threatens to abandon his bookbinding (3), reads his dirty magazines (8), complains about prank phone calls and barking dogs (2), and composes his short, sardonic poetry: "Viper in a Microwave. Sssssssssssssssssuss!!" (34). Sandra, meanwhile, grumbles about her boss (4), avoids the second floor of their home (15), and dreams of escaping (15). Their daily life seems sheltered, predictable, and (apparently) permanent.

Their relationship, however, is more than an eerie familiarity. Despite her assurances to Norman, Sandra plans, as soon as possible, to sell their house in Streatham (Kops 20), their home since childhood, because their past clearly has left its scars on them both. Sandra occasionally regresses into a childlike state while reminiscing over old photo albums (9), while Norman is more permanently stunted.[2] As Sandra mutters to herself upon Norman's pretending to sleepwalk off to bed: "A five-year-old boy, trapped in the body of a man. Unlike me, the child never escaped" (9).

The audience quickly senses that the siblings are isolated, claustrophobic, and trapped by the past (Kops 9). They mechanically finish each other's sentences. They eavesdrop. They do not so much interact with one another as perform an incestuous dance, certain (and a little fearful) that the other knows exactly what is expected.[3] Norman tells Sandra: "Don't torture yourself. When I can do it so much better for you" (9). Indeed, Sandra and Norman know each other too well, and, armed with that intimacy, depend and prey upon each other. Sandra's dream may be to escape the utter neediness of the agoraphobic Norman (28), but, as the play progresses, it seems unlikely.

Pivotal in their twisted relationship is Sinatra, the principal source of energy and primary mode of communication. He is, first and foremost, the fabric of their existence, and "playing Sinatra" is the centerpiece of their amusement. At any point, Norman can initiate or end the playacting game of Sinatra trivia. Like a child, Norman clings to this imaginary life, and, like a wearied parent, Sandra goes along for the ride, reluctantly but invariably (Kops 6–7).

Sinatra also serves as the soundtrack of their lives. They listen to him constantly and deliberately. Throughout the play, therefore, the characters continually select and play a variety of songs including "Something's Gotta Give," "Young at Heart," "Tender Trap," "Strangers in the Night," "I've Got You under My Skin," "All the Way," and "High Hopes." In every scene there is at least one Sinatra song, or—if no actual recording is played—a character inevitably alludes to the man or his music.

Through Sinatra's omnipresence, the playwright discloses how the singer's music performs multiple functions for Sandra and Norman. One important use of Sinatra by the Lewises is as the ultimate litmus test for strangers. When Sandra recounts her first meeting with Phillip de Groot, who is "obviously a man of some means . . . [who has been] travelling in Asia for some time" (Kops 11), Norman quickly asks his opinion of Sinatra. While skeptical of de Groot's rather generic response, "He's the greatest," Norman now at least has a reference point upon which he can base any further contact with the *I Ching*-quoting suitor, the first new face to enter their lives in quite a while.

Another application of Sinatra for the siblings is truly recreational, some "artificial respiration" at the end of a tiresome day (Kops 5). At the quick push of a button, even after all the day's complaints and headaches, both can sway and smile to "That Old Black Magic," for example.

For Sandra, the singer's music offers an even more crucial, indeed metaphysical, sense of renewal. Toward the beginning of Act II, when Phillip asks if he might play "You Make Me Feel So Young" on the radiogram, Sandra replies: "Often I lose all my faith. Mr. Sinatra restores it at once with a song" (Kops 24). The voice of Sinatra thus offers her a quasi-religious foundation upon which she can base her life, in which she can root herself, and from which she can carry on. Bereft of any other secure reality in which to believe, Sandra has embraced Sinatra. Unfortunately, at times, the reality of the music and its importance to her can be so overwhelming that she can no longer bear to listen (24).

Sinatra can be psychotherapeutic, as well. In response to Phillip's inquiry about seeking help for her brother, Sandra states: "Doctor Sinatra[4] is the very best medicine. He helps us enormously" (28). Psychiatrists, it must be recalled, "dissect" their patients (7). Sinatra apparently keeps Norman whole, if not sane.

Finally, Sinatra's music sometimes is employed almost oracularly, as a means of divination. In a confrontation with his new rival, Phillip, Norman turns to Sinatra's "Fools Rush In (Where Angels Fear to Tread)": "What should Mr. Sinatra offer at a time like this? . . . He knows. Frank is God" (Kops 35–36). Given their prophetic nature, Sinatra's songs can address not only life's generalities (love, loss, etc.), but also the specific circumstances of individuals' lives. Kops's irony should not go unnoticed: this is not unlike the way Phillip's favorite book, the *I Ching*, traditionally has been used.

The totemic nature of Sinatra becomes crucial for the Lewises when de Groot begins to court Sandra, since Phillip, outfitted with his oriental mysticism, threatens to destroy both the delicate balance between the siblings and their rather precarious understanding of the world around them. Their only apparent defense is Sinatra. To use Norman's terminology, just as the binding of a book "transforms" words that are "arbitrary" and "carry no weight, no real validity" into "the truth" with "authority" and "inevitability" (Kops 3), so Sinatra leads them, perhaps unconsciously, to the truth, the truth about themselves. Only through Sinatra can Sandra and Norman face their pain and their weaknesses; only through Sinatra can they confront Norman's monstrousness.

A sense of the monstrous pervades the play. Just as Norman can be an "absolute monster" (Kops 23), as Sandra tells Phillip, other monsters also "haunt" Sandra (24–25), as is made evident when she rhapsodizes over Boris Karloff's 1931 film version of *Frankenstein*, which is "fused" in her brain: "the monster, running for his life, this potent, powerful creature. When he comes across a beautiful little girl with golden hair, on a swing, singing to herself . . . It is a moment of absolute beauty. Then he rushes on, soon to be destroyed." The similarities, not only between the cinematic creature and Norman, but also between Frankenstein and Frank Sinatra, are hardly coincidental. The image of Frankenstein's monster haunts Sandra just as she says Frank's "face haunts us all" (7). And the loving, tender side of a creature so "capable of monstrous acts" compellingly reflects the very conflicted Sinatra, the artist and man, about whom so much has been written.[5] This is the Sinatra who, according to John Lahr: "[f]rom the start embraced and bullied the world as his mother had embraced and bullied him" (Lahr 8). Furthermore, as Gay Talese described in his seminal 1966 essay "Frank Sinatra Has a Cold," this contradictory nature rests at the very core of his being:

Frank Sinatra does things *personally*. At Christmas time, he will personally pick dozens of presents for his close friends and family, remembering the type of jewelry they like, their favorite colors, the sizes of their shirts and dresses . . . The same Sinatra who [does] this can, within the same hour, explode in a towering rage of intolerance should a small thing be incorrectly done for him by one of his *paisanos*. (Talese 103)

Not unlike Norman and the monster, Sinatra arguably was both "vulgar" (Kops 18) and "grand opera from the day that he was born" (24), a truly protean figure: "a man of many moods and great dimension, a man who responds instantaneously to instinct—suddenly, dramatically, wildly he responds, and nobody can predict what will follow" (Talese, "Frank Sinatra Has a Cold" 104). This intimidating and unpredictable presence, as seen and felt in the "posters and photos" hanging "all over the place" (Kops 1), looms over the action.

Sandra, of course, due to her lifetime of caring for Norman, knows firsthand how difficult it is to brave such volatility. But, up to this point, Sinatra seems to represent for her its antithesis: that escapist "dream" that "you are loved and happy and are wanted" (12). Kops, however, reveals to the audience the error of Sandra's ways when, as she's falling for Phillip, she soliloquizes about romance (and its pitfalls) in front of the mirror: "Enough of that crap, Sandra . . . Mr. de Groot is real. . . . Grow up" (17). Even in her realistically low expectations, Sandra is mistaken. Mr. de Groot is not at all genuine. He is a con man after her money, her house, anything he can get. Nor, as Sandra's words and actions throughout the play seem to imply, is the romanticism that she posits in Sinatra's music some quixotic goal. Far from some sentimental naiveté, the music is the emotional product of a complex life lived fully. As Lahr writes: "Sinatra's story is hard to keep ideal, filled as it is with brigands, barbarity, and the brutalizing compromise of himself and others."

But Sinatra kept on doing the only kind of penance he knew: singing (Lahr 82–83). In other words, those very paradoxical impulses are what make Sinatra's music so powerful, so real, and, consequently, so inescapable.

Sinatra's famous 1963 self-assessment in *Playboy* only accentuates this authenticity: "as an 18-carat manic depressive and having lived a life of violent emotional contradictions, I have an over-acute capacity for sadness as well as elation. I know what the cat who wrote the song is trying to say. I've been there—and back. I guess the audience feels it along with me. They can't help it" (Sinatra 36).[6] Far from abetting one's flight from the world, Sinatra's art forces one to tackle it, suffering and all. The question for the audience, however, remains: does Sandra ever realize this? At the play's climax, after Sandra discovers that Phillip was nothing but the con man Norman warned her he was, she leaves despite Norman's protestations that: "Frankie won't let you go. There's no future without him." In Norman's mind, "playing Sinatra" is not a game; it is not pretense. It is truth. One cannot, as Sandra suggests she has, "outgrow" Sinatra, any more than one can outgrow oneself. For Norman, they are Sinatra, and he is they.

The irony of Norman's belief is that he does not know how correct he is. The playwright himself underscores Sinatra's inescapable significance in a way his characters do not (perhaps even cannot) fully grasp. On one level, Norman and Sandra's understanding of the singer and his songs is no deeper than Phillip's obvious—and oblivious—platitudes. Earlier, Sandra even declares as beautiful Phillip's ultimate *mis*reading of Sinatra: "Playing Sinatra means you can walk out of yourself. You can fly to the stars, and dream you are loved and happy and are wanted" (Kops 12). As Kops's play makes clear, however, Sinatra does not help listeners escape from their lives, but rather forces them to confront their demons, the monsters they have created and now wish to destroy. This is similar to Roger Gilbert's argument for why Sinatra belongs in the pantheon of 1950s artists (along with Tennessee Williams, Jack Kerouac, Miles Davis, and Marlon Brando, among others) "because as a great artist he fully articulated [the] contradictions, anxieties, and ambivalences" of maculinity (Gilbert 146). The true Sinatra was never about certainty and reassurance; he was "edgy, splintered and ambiguous" (149).[7] Phillip's Sinatra, as a result, can only be a false Sinatra.

Thus, we must return to the question: does Sandra come to realize this? The matter of an epiphany for Sandra can be viewed as a matter of directorial interpretation because the audience never sees Sandra again after she walks out the door. One only can conjecture how she fares in the outside world. On the one hand, her departure might be understood as nothing more than her continued flight from the ghosts that have always haunted her; in many ways, she has resolved nothing. On the other, her act can be interpreted as the final attainment of her dream: she has gotten out. Or, as she puts it, she has "outgrown" Sinatra.

I would argue that Sandra, paradoxically, becomes a true Sinatra person in the very act of her abandoning Sinatra. What she has outgrown is not the art of Sinatra's music, but rather the variety of false significations (metaphysical, recreational, and otherwise) that she and Norman, over the course of their lives, have attached to Sinatra. By leaving Norman, Phillip, Streatham, and "playing Sinatra" behind her, that is, by daring to alter her life dramatically and completely—even in the face of a future "too terrible to contemplate" (Kops 40)—Sandra finally has lived up to one of the primary tenets of "Sinatra people": "I change things. Life has meaning. I change things" (7). Now free from the "circus" (40) she has shared with Norman all these years, Sandra is stepping fully, if uneasily, into the world—though she admits she may not succeed. In the end, however, it is all about "survival," the Sinatra quality Sandra says she loved (40).

Unlike Sandra's uncertain fate, resolution for the other two characters is sadly simple and, apparently, inevitable. Almost immediately upon Sandra's exit, Phillip arrives at the house in Streatham with an unprepared chicken for dinner (41) and instantaneously fills the void for Norman, whose nonchalance toward Phillip's presence, as described in Kops's stage directions, only accents the pernicious logic of this substitution (41). In this new relationship, Norman can dominate for the first time in his life. Still, there is little doubt that their life will continue as but an inverted rendition of the one Norman and Sandra had led for so many years. Indeed, as the curtain falls and the two men are swaying familiarly to "Young at Heart," Norman mocks Sandra's apparent shortsightedness, saying: "She thinks she can change . . . [but] nothing changes all the time" (42). So two of the players continue the game, and in their little world, indeed, there would be no future without Sinatra. Nevertheless, as Sandra's declaration of independence has intimated, in one very real sense, Norman's future holds no true Sinatra anyway. By clinging so fervently to Sinatra, he has lost the singer's essence.

It has been argued that many of the works of Bernard Kops, occasionally employing pop cultural icons, examine how characters invoke "dreams and hopes as psychological necessities in an increasingly bleak world" (Baker 234). And in *Playing Sinatra*, the playwright offers a meticulously detailed, and powerfully realized, anatomy of three individuals' desires and fears. Moreover, by integrating the music and iconography of Sinatra throughout the drama, Kops also has contributed enormously to our understanding of Sinatra's enduring cultural significance as a potent, if conflicted, symbol of innocence and power, of tenderness and violence, of the sentimental impulse and the often harsh immediacy of true art.

NOTES

1. This chapter is a revision of a presentation originally presented at the Hofstra University conference, "Frank Sinatra: The Man, The Music, The Legend," in November 1998 with scenes performed by a trio of actors from Central Connecticut State University in New Britain, CT: Assistant Professor Thom Delventhal (Norman), Jennifer Ouellette (Sandra), and Josh Palace (Phillip). I would like to thank them for their invaluable contribution in helping to bring Kops's characters so fully to life for the conference audience.

2. This emphasis on Sandra and Norman's childhood makes the motif-like use of Sinatra's "Young at Heart" especially pointed.

3. The muted incestuous impulse surfaces violently in Act II scene 2, when Sandra tries to leave and Norman emblematically rapes her (39–40).

4. One wonders if Kops here is alluding to the 1985 collection of "Doonesbury" strips entitled *That's Doctor Sinatra, You Little Bimbo,* in which Garry Trudeau satirizes Sinatra's honorary degrees and Medal of Freedom Award.

5. The monstrous dimension of the singer's character also is captured, albeit more lightheartedly, in the performance of the Sinatraesque song "Just Throw It My Way" by Oscar the Grouch on the 1993 *Sesame Street* video *Sing-Along Earth Songs.*

6. While the answers given in the 1963 *Playboy* interview are generally considered to be those of Reprise Records publicist Mike Shore and not Sinatra's, the interview nonetheless remains a valid and important interpretative document since it offers a key source for Sandra and Norman's trivia questions when "playing Sinatra."

7. Michael Nelson raises the same issue when objecting to Sinatra's placement in the "Easy Listening" section of record stores: "could anything be less easy, more unsettling than hearing Sinatra sing "One for My Baby" or "When Your Lover Has Gone" (606).

CHAPTER 9

"The Voice" in the Desert: A Quartet of Frank Revelations

"Clapton is God" is one of the classic examples of graffiti to emerge during, and in many ways to define, the rock era. This deification of the British blues guitarist reflects the rebelliousness of the youth movement so pronounced in rock music, shouted, as it were, as an assault on the cultural mores of the older generation. "We reject you, your music, and (while we're at it) your god. We've got our own," it screams.

Despite the claim of the 1980s band Art in America that a "Sinatra Serenade" would redeem us from our sins, only a very few ever have approached granting Sinatra divine status. Perhaps the closest anyone has come would be novelist William Hegner in his "frankly erotic" 1973 *roman à clef*, *King Corso*, whose main character—the singer/actor/show biz monarch Jimmy Corso—is a "Dali-like deity" (10) who "shared initials with Jesus Christ" (12). Backed by a horn section of "Gabriellan purity and clarity" (11), he brings to his retirement concert a presence and force that rival the creation of Holy Scripture: "It was the way the beginning must have been. Light, intense but hazy, surrounding him, the forest primeval somewhere in the darkness beyond it" (9). When J.C. first walks on stage, the novelist even quotes

Genesis: "Let the waters under the heavens be gathered together unto one place" (Hegner 10).

Hegner employs such images for two reasons. First, and most importantly, they suit so nicely the overwrought prose of the paperback genre; and second, such spiritual language allows for the occasional ironic counterpoint to the intimate details of J.C.'s life of the flesh that are the real focus (and attraction) of the tale. How else to explain a passage such as:

God created man in his own image.

He stood there over the marble bowl urinating, naked except for his support hose, his vision wavering as it cascaded over the hill of his abdomen, the years suddenly flowing yellow and diminishing, here and there a glimmer of lost luster, the softness of his penis a reminder of schedules no longer met, of liaisons difficult to keep, the grip of his hand loose and gentle out of respect for the pleasures that it had brought him. (Hegner 48)

God becomes man indeed.

The next closest approximation of Sinatra to the Clapton credo is the one in the introduction of Sinatra at the 1995 Grammy Awards ceremony by Paul "Bono" Hewson, the lead singer of the Irish rock band U2, when he declared the singer was "living proof that God was a Catholic" (Vare 214). While far from "Sinatra is God," the religio-political ramifications of this proof, especially when uttered by an Irishman, probably tend toward a battle cry of some kind, but that is another story. Nevertheless, while rarely being equated with God, Sinatra's theological and philosophical implications have not been overlooked,[1] and this chapter will discuss a quartet of works and the ways in which their conceptions of "Frank Sinatra" grapple with such issues.

In his short story, "Commandments," Neil A. Shurley creates a Frank Sinatra of biblical proportions through the extensive use of allusion to the first two books of the Pentateuch. Invoking the basic thematic and narrative structures of Exodus, as well as a variety of powerful images from Genesis and Exodus, the 1996 short story depicts a complex Sinatra who ironically encompasses both the theophanic and the profane. Sinatra's portrayal, for example, not only mirrors Yahweh's gift of the Decalogue to Moses on Mt. Sinai, but also curiously refracts the story of Abraham's near-sacrifice of his son, Isaac. In a similar vein, Gerald Early in "Listening to Frank Sinatra" offers an almost divinely curative Sinatra who calls people to a deeper and truer knowledge of the human condition. Meanwhile, David Lloyd in "The Heavens" and

Paul Fericano in "SINATRA, SINATRA: The Poem" invoke Sinatra's name and familiar image to critique an American culture void of metaphysical reflection and quick to apotheosize celebrity.

"Commandments," set at the Stardust Casino in Las Vegas at the height of the "Rat Pack" era during the late 1950s and early 1960s, details a brief fictional backstage encounter of Sinatra with a cocktail waitress mother and her catechism student son. The waitress, who is summoned by the performer after his set, surprises him (and thwarts his obvious intentions) by bringing to Sinatra's dressing room her youngster, armed with his newly memorized "Ten Commandments." The frustrated and, to some degree, bemused singer consequently engages the young boy in his own version of religious education concluding with "the eleventh commandment," "Thou shalt stick to your mother like glue," then waves them both away. Thus, the religious faith and maternal love of the waitress help to transform the temptation of and possible threat to the woman's virtue into a revelatory opportunity for all three characters.

The story, a childhood memory narrated by the grown-up son, relates when he and his mother lived in Vegas before he was old enough to enter school. The waitress, to reward her son for learning the week's Bible verses from his "Beginning Christians" class, would allow him to watch the shows with the guy in the light booth. "Eddie," of course, offered the lad a very different education from that provided by his mother: "he knew all [the] moves" of the singers, the comedians, and the magicians who headlined night after night (Shurley 61). This education clearly went beyond show business, since he told the boy stories that he must "swear never to tell your mother" (61). Of quite contrary kinds, to be sure, but this boy was fully engaged in learning.[2]

And it is in the curious world of that oasis, Las Vegas, where the sacred and the profane intersect so intimately, that Sinatra dwells like Yahweh atop Mount Sinai. His extraordinary status, after all, is recognized already by the boy since Sinatra is the only entertainer through whose set even the irreverent Eddie remains silent; instead, he sits "mesmerized as Sinatra worked the room" (61). Even his mother had dressed him in his "Sunday morning bow tie" for this performance (61).

Thus, when Sinatra summons the mother after the show, via a "large man in a small suit . . . grinning menacingly" (61), there is an obvious apprehension about the "demand": "She blushed, hesitating, then patted her hair in place and motioned for me to follow her" (61). Unaware of the real nature of the invitation, of course, the boy nonetheless

grasps immediately the power and authority the singer wields, and stepping into his dressing room means entering a very different world.

The concept of being summoned, of receiving the divine call and
one's response to it, is central to the action of the scriptural Pentateuch,
and Shurley takes full advantage of the themes by playing upon both the
biblical stories of both Abraham and Moses. But, unlike the familiar
story from Genesis of Abraham's faithful, but reluctant, near-sacrifice
of his son at the behest of the Lord, the mother here brings her child in
defense and defiance of the call. Instead of the sacrificial victim, who is
to be offered but spared in the end, the son serves as the shield against
sin. If Isaac is proof of Abraham's faith in God, the son in "Commandments" is a weapon against temptation.

In one way, her hiding behind the child—"Mother stood . . . still
holding me in front of her" (Shurley 61)—seems an utterly selfish and
cowardly act. Unwilling to offer herself, unwilling to sacrifice her own
probity, she depends upon the innocence of her son to protect them
both. An even less flattering view of the mother might be the boy's being considered as but her safeguard against her own weaknesses; unable
to resist Sinatra herself, she makes her child the fortification she herself
cannot breach. Far more the focus, however, are the woman's basic
goodness and foresight. Her interest in the religious education of her
son clearly argues for a parent intent on raising a young man who knows
the difference between right and wrong. Her ability to recognize what
the summons from Sinatra entails also indicates a woman who is not
naïve; she knows the landscape well enough to navigate it successfully.
(Of course, the nature of her previous experience and education is unclear, although perhaps her raising the boy alone suggests a wisdom ac-
quired the hard way.)

Most illustrative of the mother's decency, however, is how well the
boy behaves and performs. He is invariably obedient, courteous, and
intelligent, in the most unfeigned and spontaneous way. His genuine-
ness, for example, is highlighted when the singer, even as "his eyes
locked with mother's," casually inquires, "Whattaya know, kid?" and
the boy surprises him with a hesitating but forthright answer, "The Ten
Commandments, sir" (Shurley 61). And from this point on, by his di-
verting Sinatra's attention from the frustrated intent of his invitation,
the boy, rather than Sinatra or the mother, dictates the remainder of the
encounter. For when the boy begins to answer Sinatra's "Ten Commandments" quiz correctly, Sinatra replies, "That's good. You're a smart
kid" (Shurley 62).

This benediction by Sinatra then ushers in the revelation of the eleventh commandment and the parallel to the biblical story of Moses on Mt. Sinai. If the boy had been less authentic or impressive, his mother and he would have faced a quick, angry dismissal (or worse). Thus, instead of bearing the brunt of an anger born of unfulfilled desire, the boy and his mother are blessed with Sinatra's grace, an utterly unexpected gift (the basic meaning of the Latin *gratia*) from the singer. Sinatra's commandment, "Thou shalt stick to your mother like glue" (62), in fact, pays as much of a compliment to the mother as it does to the boy, since it powerfully affirms the way she has raised him. As Sinatra says approvingly in "dismiss[ing them] with a wave of his hand," "You've got a smart kid there, doll" (Shurley 62). As the Israelites received the Lord's blessing for the faithful execution of His commands by Abraham and Moses, so the mother and child are rewarded with an epiphany of their own.

Obviously, the act of giving the boy an eleventh commandment, to complement the ten he already has learned from his mother, equates Sinatra directly with the Yahweh of Exodus. His powerful and mysterious presence is decidedly god-like, and Shurley evokes the Hebrew text throughout, on the level of both image and theme. The education of the boy (by both his mother and Eddie), for example, parallels the education of Moses as presented in Exodus 2.[3] Even more immediately, however, Shurley employs smoke to create in Sinatra's dressing room an atmosphere quite reminiscent of Mt. Sinai. In Exodus, for example, Yahweh tells Moses: "Lo, I am coming to you in a thick cloud" (19:9) and, on the third day, "Mount Sinai was wrapped in smoke, because the Lord descended upon it in fire; and the smoke of it went up like smoke of a kiln, and the whole mountain quaked greatly" (19:18). In "Commandments," smoke also dominates the narrator's memory of Sinatra's dressing room: "Sinatra sat at a dressing table, his back to us, smoking a cigarette (Shurley 61). He took another drag (61). He smashed his cigarette into an ashtray, causing one last trail of smoke to curl upward (61). His breath smelled of smoke and whiskey" (62). He shoved me away and lit another cigarette" (62). Punctuating Sinatra's every move, smoke serves as a scriptural veil that shrouds the singer from the boy while simultaneously dazzling him.

Most importantly, however, the short story parallels Exodus by focusing its thematic attention upon the revelation of the divine figure. As Exodus concentrates on the revelation of the identity of Yahweh, so "Commandments" details the revelation of Sinatra's self to the boy and his mother. And just as Yahweh's name, which means "I AM THAT I AM," embodies "a paradox of absolute being and involvement" (Fokkelman 63), so Sinatra's self-revelation is paradoxical at its core, as well. More than any other characteristic, readers sense Sinatra's love and respect for his own mother, Dolly, whose influence on and support of her son is almost legendary.[4] This profound dedication to his mother (as awkward as it may seem when juxtaposed to his lecherous, and perhaps misogynistic, approach toward women in the story) is a pivotal, if paradoxical, element of his character. Sinatra, ironically, embodies not only divine attributes, but the profane also. He is the corrupting force in the tale; he is the evil to be defeated or, at the very least, kept at bay. His command for the woman to appear, after all, is only to satisfy the basest of carnal desires; he is temptation (and imminent peril) incarnate.[5] Of course, this combination of temptation[6] and grace, of imminent danger and divine immanence, is what makes Shurley's Sinatra so compelling. The intimate proximity of this omnipotent being is simultaneously his most attractive and threatening characteristic. He demands acquiescence, and his presence urges its immediate compliance even as he reveals deep-seated nurturing and protective impulses.

Libertine and faithful son, miscreant and demi-god, Sinatra's very inconsistencies as described by Shurley suggest a figure of mythical proportion.[7] And if mythology is, at its root, the attempt to delineate the boundaries between the divine and the mortal, then such stories of the Rat Pack era (with their made-for-HBO cast of legendary figures like the Kennedys, Marilyn Monroe, Sam Giancana, etc. certainly conjure up a mythic Golden Age, reminiscent of Hesiod and Ovid, when immortals still walked upon the Earth . . . as Sinatra, Jove-like, lords over the action.

The ability to hear—and accept—the power of Sinatra's voice is also central to Gerald Early's 1989 poem "Listening to Frank Sinatra," in which even the most tender emotions at the heart of Sinatra's songs of love and loss can touch the so-called "horror of horrors" (15), the hideous sideshow freak condemned to live with a bag over his head. As characterized in Early's poem, the singer calls everyone to understand the human condition and, in doing so, helps them to "make it through the day" (47).

In the poem, the speaker recalls a pivotal childhood experience at a carnival when the sideshow "star," in answer to the question of what he did all day, responded:

> Why listen to Frank Sinatra, as if *that* was,
> As if everyone should or would do what was the
> Naturalest thing in the whole wide world. (22–24)

Even as a boy, the speaker was struck not primarily by the grotesque face that made the man the main attraction, but by his simple revelation that "Listening to Frank Sinatra gets you through the day" (36). After all, as the boy would ponder later:

> what could he know
> Of Frank Sinatra, of sitting with a girl in
> A darkened room, kissing wet kisses. (29–31)

But that apparent chasm between Frank Sinatra and the sideshow mutant, between connection and isolation, is what he comes to recognize makes Sinatra so remarkable, so important. For, as the man now tells his children:

> if Frank Sinatra could
> Do so much for the man who was the horror of horrors,
> To sing such that he could make it through a day
> Just think what such listening can do for me. (45–48)

Sinatra touches everyone who listens to him. Like the sick, blind, and lame who, in faith and hope, reached out but to touch the cloak of Jesus and found themselves healed, so the speaker sees the profound relief that Sinatra offers to even the most marginalized individuals in society. And now, as a disciple who has witnessed the curative power of the singer and his songs, he preaches the good news of Sinatra.

Of course, prophets have learned throughout the ages that always accompanying the vocation is the danger inherent in accepting and responding to a call that not everyone has heard. For, inevitably, it leads to ridicule by those who will not or cannot open themselves up to the message. His children, for example, are quite puzzled and embarrassed by a father who:

> keeps straining to hear Frank Sinatra off
> Somewhere on a PA or someone's radio . . . to
> Hear Frank Sinatra where there is no Frank Sinatra
> Where no one else wants to hear Frank Sinatra at all. (39–40; 42–43)

But he now is a true believer, an apostle who cannot but act upon the conviction that no matter how popular, no matter how solitary a life one may be forced to lead, Sinatra's songs somehow can touch that life actively and meaningfully. All one needs to do is to heed his call.

If, in Shurley's fiction and Early's poem, Sinatra and his art are represented as an almost divine calling that alters one's life and world, a decidedly more finite Sinatra is found in David Lloyd's lyric, "The Heavens." While his Sinatra ponders the metaphysical questions that, over the course of history, have troubled humankind, he is ultimately frustrated in his attempts; for, in Las Vegas, there can be "no revelations beyond what revolving numbers can tell" (23).

Here is the poem, in full:

The Heavens

All the moths of Nevada seek out
these infamous lights, immolating themselves
in countless sparks on the "S" and the "d" of the Sands Casino.

With all the shuffling, rolling, clanking   5
money machines, the infinite décolletage
and spinning ice cubes, the smoke
and the mirrors, no one sees
this dusty descent of bodies and wings,
antennae and legs, the steady yearning,   10
the tiny deaths that don't stop.

No one sees, that is, but Frank,
staring up from the balcony of his three-bedroom,
second-floor suite, cigarette poised between fingers,
a Jack Daniels on the rocks with a twist   15
and a swizzle at the ready.

Where do they come from? he asks out loud,
as if a flunky with an answer was waiting.
Why, he wants to know, *don't they stop?*
Frank leans further out and squints.   20
But no stars dot this desert sky. No meteors
beginning somewhere, ending elsewhere.
No revelations beyond what revolving numbers can tell.
Here, the earth casts its brilliant shadow
over all the heavens, everywhere and forever.   25

Frank shrugs his shoulders,
checks his watch, tightens the knot
of his tie, flicks a half-inch of ash
over the railing for the desert breeze to dissect.
Downstairs, the Copa waits.   30

In both its characterizations of Sinatra's listeners and the entertainer himself, Lloyd's poem is a breed apart from Early's. Distracted by the lights and noise of Las Vegas and drawn like "all the moths of Nevada" to the neon "S" and "d" (1–3), the fans swarm to the desert instinctively, utterly without reflection. Indeed, the call to which they seem to respond has little in common with Shurley's summons to Sinai or even Early's invitation to community. Instead, Lloyd offers people, incapable of a deeper understanding of themselves as either individuals or more collectively as humans and drawn blissfully to die in the desert, who are content just to be near such a luminary as Sinatra. As powerful an attraction as he may be to them, however, they remain powerless to take away anything substantial or uplifting from his art.

Another significant departure is the performer himself. As the poem makes clear, only Sinatra is sensitive enough to raise the metaphysical question of "why?"[8] Unfortunately, even he remains too earthbound, too tied—almost too central—to American culture to formulate an answer. While it is Sinatra alone who raises the questions, "Where do they come from?" (17) and "Why don't they stop?" (19), even he finally must abandon the search because "Downstairs the Copa waits" (30). Always able to perform for the masses, the singer nevertheless seems silenced by the gilded cage in which he finds himself. In the end, while Frank may attempt to understand the apparently universal self-destructive impulses that no one else notices, he cannot arrive at an adequate or plausible answer. To make matters worse, Lloyd's poem suggests that, even if Sinatra would reach such an answer, the audience probably would neither comprehend nor care about it.

An artist who apparently senses the right questions to consider but who cannot resolve them successfully, Lloyd's Sinatra, in the end, is himself at risk in the neon-lit desert. He alone may make the effort to "lean further out and squint" at the stars in the sky (20), but it is his, as much as the Earth's, presence that casts such an imposing shadow and blots them out. Incapable of breaking free from the world he has helped to create, Sinatra, as both moth and flame, cannot but abandon his quest or risk destroying himself in the process. As the poem suggests in the shrug of the singer's shoulders and his habitual gestures of straightening his tie and checking the time (26–28), his choice is sadly clear. When the Copa is waiting downstairs, the heavens can wait.

As long as the shadow that Sinatra casts over "The Heavens" may be, however, the entertainer possesses an even more profound presence in Paul Fericano's "SINATRA, SINATRA: The Poem." With a ubiquity that produces a Sinatra as imposing and inescapable as American culture itself and, simultaneously, that so abstracts him as to make him a cipher, the satirist finds that eventually everything comes up "sinatra."

In his thirty-six-line satire, a litany of "prepared statement[s]" (13), "stupid assertion[s]" (24), and "violent persuasion[s]" (7), Fericano places the Sinatra name in a variety of contexts—often with hilariously pointed results. In eleven of the twelve stanzas, he makes "sinatra" the subject or direct object of the assertion or query, from an array of fields including economics, politics, medicine, and nuclear strategy.

Interestingly, Fericano's juxtaposition of "sinatra" with such adjectives as "malignant" (5) and "sawed-off" (8) gives the satire its bite not, as one expects, because of the unexpected and comic nature of the resulting combinations. Instead, their power stems from the extraordinary synergy that derives from their familiar and pervasive roots in the Sinatra legend. The biographical details and psychological truths the public feels that they know about Sinatra make everything from a "supply-side sinatra" (17) to the ithyphallic "protruding sinatra" (2)[9] remarkably familiar. Who, after all, could deny the "real" Sinatra's phenomenal success in both the economic and erotic worlds? Everything that the public has read, heard, or imagined about Sinatra tells them that, financially and romantically, he lived the life all men should long to live. The oft-told tales of his mob ties also make "organized sinatra" (12) an almost natural phrase. And his well-documented temper and severe distrust of the press are captured by the:

> Prepared statement:
> Kiss my sinatra.
> Blow it out your sinatra. (13–15)

Likewise, his connections to the White House (most prominently with Kennedy and Reagan) add to the plausibility of such combinations as "The sinatra stops here" (19), a twist on the famous motto of Harry Truman, and "limited nuclear sinatra" (23), a phrase eerily common during the cold war.[10] In short, the Sinatra of tabloid and unauthorized biographies is as multifarious and omnipresent as Fericano's "sinatra" is, and the poem makes a telling point about such a correspondence.[11]

As the final stanza offers the "Biblical fact" that "Man does not live by sinatra alone" (35–36), the ability of the satire to make even the most absurd "reflections" plausible powerfully refutes the scriptural verse. After all, in its endless and apparently unappeasable worship of celebrities like Sinatra, America has existed precisely that way over the years, and the poem suggests that "Frank Sinatra," as brand name and commercial icon, repeatedly has shown itself expansive and resilient enough to satisfy ably the popular demands:

> Sinatra this, sinatra that.
> Sinatra do, sinatra don't.
> Sinatra come, sinatra go. (28–30)

And the American public, no longer willing to relegate pop figures to secular culture, has chosen to apotheosize such individuals as Sinatra and to sacrifice at their altars. In America, remember, even Mary is "full of sinatra" (26).

With so ubiquitous and formidable a presence as "sinatra" confronting him, the poet must ask whether there is a place for anyone, anything else. Thus, the only stanza that does not include the name is the penultimate one, which asks a "historical question":

> Is the poet who wrote this poem
> still alive? (32–34)

The question implies that, with so many sinatras so ever- and omnipresent, things that should matter, like poetry (and the lives of the artists who create it), necessarily go unnoticed—to the ultimate detriment of the culture. Similar to Lloyd's poem, then, Fericano critiques the simplemindedness of an omnivorous celebrity culture and its disinterest, even hostility, to matters of real consequence.

With very few exceptions, then, there has been no secular figure that has offered a more inviting canvas for religious representation than Sinatra has: God and Satan, healer and plague, savior and false idol. And that writers like Early, Fericano, Lloyd, and Shurley can make such disparate use of the image and name argues much for Sinatra's essential cultural significance. It, of course, is not that the historical Sinatra, as it were, was either godlike or the devil incarnate, but rather that the many facets of his long and intimately familiar life were so readily adaptable to traditionally mythic narrative settings. In everything from his commanding, ineffable presence and Zeus-like womanizing to his martyrdom at Ava's altar of love and the "resurrection" of his career, Sinatra's legends only seem to reiterate the fundamental beliefs—of sacrifice, redemption, and the glories that can arise from even the most humble of births—upon which so much of American myth is based. If Graceland, as Paul Simon suggests, is the pop pilgrim's destination of choice, then it is the "Book of Frank" which must be viewed as the most sacred of

American texts. Sinatra's story (more so than that of Elvis, Jackie O, or even Marilyn) invariably raises the most fundamental questions of damnation and deliverance, and through its continued explication is generated an increasingly rich understanding of what America is and means.

NOTES

1. See Edmund Santurri's intriguing "Theology and Music in a Different Key: Frank Sinatra in a Fallen World" in *Frank Sinatra and Popular Culture: Essays on an American Icon.*

2. The 2000 film *What Women Want* offers a contrasting perspective on a son's growing up with a working Vegas mom. Mel Gibson's Nick Marshall is a "man's man": the kind of man who thinks he is God's gift to women, the kind of man other men want to emulate. He is also the kind of man who views Sinatra, in this age of women's empowerment, as the ultimate "antidote to estrogen." Thus, when facing a serious career challenge from Helen Hunt's Darcy McGuire, he turns to wine and music to escape his troubles and ends up dancing solo (except for a black fedora and a coat rack) through his Chicago bachelor pad to Sinatra's 1956 recording of "I Won't Dance." The Nancy Meyers film as a whole, however, suggests a far less chauvinistic appreciation of Sinatra with his classic version of "I've Got You under My Skin" underscoring the late night office scene in which Nick and Darcy first begin falling in love. The soundtrack also contains Sinatra's recording of "Too Marvelous for Words" and a soundtrack full of songs and singers intimately connected with the singer.

3. The short story also echoes the development of Exodus with its combination of two different emphases: the narrative and the normative, the presentation of the story itself and the rules by which to live (Fokkelman 56).

4. As Alan King writes about Frank: "He always said of his own mother that she was his best pal" (114).

5. This same hellish facet of Sinatra's larger-than-life persona has been exploited both by Frank himself in "What Time Does the Next Miracle Leave?" (see chapter 5), and by Al Pacino's John Milton—aka Satan—in the climactic scene of 1997's *Devil's Advocate*, when he finally discloses to his son his true identity (in all its awesome and timeless power) while playfully lip-synching to Sinatra's 1956 recording of "It Happened in Monterey."

6. In some versions of Exodus, due to the blending of different textual traditions, Yahweh seems to do His own bit of tempting as well. Moses, for instance, seemingly must remind the Lord of His own explicit orders to "set bounds for the people . . . to not go up into the mountain or touch the border of it" (19:12) when the deity suggests that the priests "who come near" should consecrate themselves (19:23).

7. In his brief autobiographical essay, "Saint Francis," Vincent Zangrillo offers a similar take on the complex nature of Sinatra's canonization.

8. Lloyd is not alone in granting a truly cerebral dimension to Sinatra. In the notes to his "Love in the Western World: Sinatra and the Conflict of Generations," T.H. Adamowski briefly compares Sinatra and Sartre (36–37). And through cameo appearances in his panoramic novel, *City of God*, E.L. Doctorow places Sinatra on an analogous plane with such scientific and philosophical heavyweights as Einstein and Wittgenstein (223–232).

9. On his late-1960s album, *Don Rickles Speaks!*, the comedian jokes that Sinatra's next spouse, if the singer ever should decide to remarry, would have to be an animal since he already had exhausted every other erotic possibility. Even Sinatra himself seemed not to shy away from this aspect of his public persona. During the January 24, 1958, episode of his ABC television show, *The Frank Sinatra Show*, on which he and Jo Stafford reminisce about their days with Tommy Dorsey, Sinatra jokes about his far-from-ascetic lifestyle that clearly dated back at least to the early 1940s. In October 1946, he recorded the Cahn and Styne song from *Ladies' Man*, "I Got a Gal I Love (in North and South Dakota)." And, as producer of the four 1963 *Reprise Musical Repertory Theatre* records, he assigned himself the lecherous leprechaun's song, "When I'm Not Near the Girl I Love (I Love the Girl I'm Near)," from *Finian's Rainbow*, while passing along the *Kiss Me Kate* song of lost bachelorhood, "Where Is the Life That Late I Led," to Lou Monte.

10. In Michael Ventura's *The Death of Frank Sinatra*, the Las Vegas private investigator Mike Rose makes a comparable connection between nuclear capability and the singer due to Sinatra's ownership of a company that makes guided missile parts (224–225). See chapter 10.

11. Consider David Letterman's "Top Ten Signs That Your Wife Is Seeing Sinatra" which still depicts Sinatra, at the age of eighty, as a sexually potent and eminently dangerous rake. In 1946, when T-Bone Walker recorded "Bobby Sox Blues," Sinatra as a romantic rival was credible and, given the intensity of "Sinatrauma," quite accurate, but that the identical image is still viable in 1995, even in a comic setting, is a remarkable testament to Sinatra's staying power.

CHAPTER **10**

Tales of Two Cities:
Sinatra as *Genius Hobokenensis*
and Vegas Incarnate

Countless songs have been written about cities, but only a very few of these songs are intimately and incontrovertibly identified with specific performers.[1] For instance, it will always be Judy Garland who is to meet Louis in St. Louis, Tony Bennett who leaves his heart in San Francisco, and Randy Newman[2] who loves L.A. This rare connection of singer, song, and city makes Frank Sinatra's musical connections not only to the Big Apple (in both Comden and Green's 1949 "New York, New York" and his 1979 recording of Kander and Ebb's identically titled song),[3] but also to the Windy City (in "Chicago" and "My Kind of Town," not to mention its south side in "Bad, Bad, Leroy Brown") all the more remarkable.[4]

Even more striking is that Sinatra's intimate associations with another pair of U.S. cities have required no specific songs at all. Even nonfans know of his Hoboken roots, and Las Vegas and Sinatra seem inseparable in the public consciousness, as well. Gay Talese acknowledges these bonds in his classic 1966 *Esquire* profile, "Frank Sinatra Has a Cold," for example, which seeks to evoke the essence of both locations (along with Hollywood and New York City) in its attempt to capture the man and his influence. And it is his close affiliations with Hoboken, New Jersey, and Las Vegas, Nevada, that authors Ed Shirak, Jr., and Michael Ventura exploit in their respective books, the memoir *Our Way* and the detective novel *The Death of Frank Sinatra*. While Hoboken and Vegas may be quite different cities and the books two decidedly different genres, in each case the city is but the man writ large—albeit only a wee bit larger since the man is Sinatra.

AT PLAY IN THE FIELDS OF FRANK

At its foundation, Ed Shirak, Jr.'s 1995 memoir *Our Way* must be read as a gloss on a photograph of a young Frank Sinatra sitting on a Hoboken pier. For in the murky photograph, the author perceives the perfect likeness of the grand dreams inherent in both the singer-to-be and the New Jersey city. That the pier also was part of the Elysian Fields, the historically significant sight of the first organized baseball game, makes the picture all the more "mystical" for Shirak because in his mystic Hoboken, over which the spirits of baseball and Sinatra hover like Roman *genii*, miraculous events do occur. Indeed, Shirak would like the reader to consider *Our Way* itself—with its vivid portrayal of the portentous convergence of baseball, Sinatra, and the dreams of an ordinary man—as one such Hoboken miracle.[5] It is all in the picture.

As the title suggests, the memoir intends to champion the honor and spirit of the people of Hoboken, who were maligned by what they refer to only as "that book," Kitty Kelly's 1986 *His Way: The Unauthorized Biography of Frank Sinatra*.[6] Written to set straight the record that Kelly in her "first 44 pages" either misunderstood or misrepresented, *Our Way* nevertheless spends most of its effort recounting the author's quest to honor the singer appropriately. Consequently, it centers on Shirak's frustrated attempts to present Sinatra personally with the tribute song that he has produced, "The Time That Was." The book then carefully details the series of personal and professional setbacks that prevent the meeting from occurring, including a warning from syndicated radio host Sid Mark that "No one gets to Sinatra not even me anymore" (2), despite which Shirak carries on.[7] Even at the conclusion of the book, after delivering the song to the very door of Sinatra's suite at the Sands Hotel in Atlantic City, the author cannot be sure that the singer has received his gift, and his uncertainty thus serves as the impetus for the book. (In fact, only two days *after* the private publication of *Our Way*, Shirak would receive a note of thanks from Sinatra, the "miraculous" news of which is revealed in a photocopied addendum inserted in the book and more fully rehearsed on a cassette tape accompanying the book and including "The Time That Was." The miracle of *Our Way* is thus fulfilled.) At times, then, given the author's dominant role in his narrative, it may seem difficult to discern the collective nature of *Our Way*, but the people of Hoboken are very much at its core.

Like Michael Moore's 1989 documentary, *Roger and Me*, which recounts the filmmaker's attempts (on the behalf of the laid-off auto workers of Flint, Michigan) to meet with General Motors CEO Roger Smith, *Our Way* depicts a man's often solitary and, some might say, daft actions in the interests of his community. However, unlike Moore's satiric take on his target and even himself, at times, Shirak depicts a world in which, armed with a desire to pay tribute to the "greatest performer in the world" (Shirak 18) and empowered by the profound words of St. Peter (2), John Paul II (2), and Eleanor Roosevelt (4), among others, he is an earnestly somber crusader for his city.

As a result, the basic sincerity of the author should not be questioned. Of course, any book in which an author recounts in detail both his failed bid for mayor and his conviction for driving while intoxicated must be considered self-serving to some degree, but Shirak's quest—to help revive Hoboken by building the "From Here to Eternity" hotel on the sight of an abandoned Maxwell House Coffee plant—also must be deemed noble, if somewhat quixotic. As a result, although Shirak originally intended *Our Way* as an homage to Sinatra, it might be better understood as a love song to Hoboken and its people. For Hoboken's past is repeatedly invoked as the ultimate inspiration for Sinatra (as well as Shirak himself). In his "Author's Note," for example, Shirak admits that Sinatra's talent was "God given," but his narrative also makes manifest that Sinatra was undeniably a product of Hoboken, the town that also gave the world baseball (Shirak 10), many of Stephen Foster's greatest songs (16), and the first screw propeller steamboat (115). To Shirak, any attempt to distinguish the town and the singer is bound to be futile.[8] Consequently, to recognize Hoboken's favorite and most famous son is necessarily to celebrate the rich history of the city.

Shirak's effective equation of Sinatra's past with Hoboken's history is but one part of the calculus of the book, however. The present and the future of Hoboken also must be factored in, and Shirak offers his life in and experience of Hoboken as the final variable. This reading of the work helps to explain the author's rather digressive narrative style that incorporates a variety of tangential issues, including his own sociopolitical beliefs, into what should be a fairly straightforward tale. At the beginning of chapter 6, for example, after the loss of both the

Hoboken mayoral election and his life savings, Shirak briefly recounts another (losing) battle, this one resulting from the high cost of medical treatment for a bee sting to Mario Lepore, his partner (Shirak 60–61).

Such parentheses as this argue that the book hopes, as much as anything, to capture the tough-minded spirit of Hoboken, which Shirak himself describes as a "blue collar," "ethnic," and "family" town (94–95). Indeed, chapter 8 is devoted entirely to the voices of the people of Hoboken, some of whom were interviewed by Kitty Kelly for *His Way*, so that they might retell "their story," this time accurately (96). *Our Way* thus metamorphoses from a salute to a local-boy-made-great into a story of ordinary people who—and this condition is key to Shirak's worldview—*if* given the opportunity and a level playing field, can achieve extraordinary things. Such a philosophy also explains the presence of populist political statements including a pair of cartoons by Mario Lepore on the ill-treatment of the middle class (41, 61) and passages such as: "The greed of the Hospitals and insurance companies is why 40 million Americans do not have health insurance" (60), and "The Federal Government uses the inflation myth to raise the prime rate, which punishes what is left of the middle class so Washington can lend 20 billion dollars to Mexico when no Latin loan has been repaid since 1800" (62). The focus on ordinary people/extraordinary achievements also partially explains why chapter 1 commences with a brief look at the author's family history.

Shirak begins with the story of his uncle, James Vincent Galante, a decorated soldier in World War II, whose photographs of a young Sinatra (including the one on the pier) inspire the hotel and the song that will anchor the plot of *Our Way*. But war hero Uncle Jimmy's story also serves as the author's rejoinder to such people as Stephen Speiser, the lawyer/head of the American Heritage Baseball Association who had dismissed Shirak and his efforts because he "had no letter head," or, as Shirak translates it, because he lacked: "the legal clout [lawyers and politicians] possess in a seal to get things accomplished that, in their view, an ordinary person can not achieve"[9] (11). In short, people like his uncle saved their country and the world; no idea is too big for Hoboken, which is something Shirak feels people too easily forget.

It is this fighting spirit of Hoboken, what the Romans might have called the *genius* of the place, that unifies Shirak's often-unwieldy narrative. Just as the Romans could recognize and celebrate the "unity and continuity underlying successive generations" of a single family (and, later, of any group joined by a common interest) as its particular *genius* (Barrow 20), so Shirak's book displays the *genius* of Hoboken, the "mysterious extra," the defining spirit that makes the city, its people, and its past unique. Uncle Jimmy offers but one example of the Hoboken *genius* at work; baseball and Sinatra offer readers two more.

The Sinatra saga begins in earnest in chapter 2, with Shirak's first crusade: his attempt to gain more complete recognition for Hoboken as the birthplace of baseball. As the head of the city's Babe Ruth League, the author had been invited by the mayor to participate in the city's first "Baseball Day Celebration," which would commemorate the first organized baseball game on June 19, 1846, at the Elysian Fields in Hoboken (10). As Shirak writes: "I wanted to do more than just participate in Baseball Day and decided Hoboken should have a Baseball tribute song" (10). Not coincidentally, he was managing a singer/songwriter, Jimmy Reardon, who then proceeded to write and record "Baseball Was Born in This Town," the title of which was Shirak's idea (11).

From this point on, Shirak begins to recount the obstacles to his vision that the rest of his story will relate repeatedly. He meets with the "arrogance and resistance" (11) of the people in charge, until finally Reardon, in fact, performs the song on Baseball Day in front of the governor of New Jersey and a variety of baseball dignitaries, such as Bobby Thomson (12). Shirak views this first achievement, however, as only a qualified success since he had agreed to let the mayor "commission" the song, which "translated politically . . . meant City Hall created the idea to have a baseball tribute song" (12) and not Shirak himself. In short, he receives no formal recognition, although he does not hesitate to point out that, within weeks, Jimmy Reardon, his client would be performing for "Tony Bennett, who is Mr. Sinatra's favorite singer, at the posh supper club, On the Waterfront in Hoboken. . . . In 1952, scenes from the academy award winning movie, "On the Waterfront" were filmed at the bar starring Marlon Brando and Eva Marie Saint" (12). Performing in front of Governor Florio is one thing, Shirak clearly is suggesting, but singing for Tony Bennett is in a whole other league.

The previous passage is also emblematic of Shirak's approach to telling his story.[10] In the space of two sentences, while trying to set the record straight concerning his integral role in a major public event, he has linked himself, through Bennett and Reardon, directly to both Sinatra and an appropriately historic moment for Hoboken. He may not have letterhead (as he describes himself), but these connections clearly suggest that he possesses what it takes to be a public force nonetheless.

In similar fashion, Shirak redefines and, in a sense, redeems himself and his city in the eyes of others simply by mentioning Sinatra's Hoboken roots. For example, when he joins Church and Dwight, Inc., in New York City as a Corporate Employment Manager, and people ask where he is from, his straightforward answer of Hoboken is met only with derision. However, when he begins answering "Hoboken, home of Frank Sinatra," he becomes "accepted by my peers as well as my superiors" (94). It is precisely this type of reaction to Hoboken, in general, and Shirak, in particular, the book means to encourage. The Sinatra-Hoboken link is so strong that dismissing the city (and its residents) is paramount to dismissing the singer himself. The world at large only needs to recognize the close kinship of the town and the star finally to grant the "historic city" its due (94).

The author turns his attention to honoring Sinatra in a way that would be both suitable for such a larger-than-life individual and helpful to the people of Hoboken. Inspired by one of his uncle's old photographs of Sinatra, in which the young man sits "staring mystically across the Hudson" from the pier at old Elysian Field (20), Shirak begins envisioning building "From Here to Eternity": "a hotel on the Hudson . . . which would include a Sinatra theatre for the performing arts along with a special site for Baseball's Hall of Fame since baseball was born in this town" (Shirak 21). That the idea is a grand one does not escape him, but his language is almost Homeric in its psychology when he writes that "the idea took hold in my mind" (21). And almost as if the idea is a separate entity, it consumes him (and his bank account). He finally settles, however, on the more modest idea of producing a Sinatra tribute song, "A Time That Was," and delivering it personally to Mr. Sinatra.[11]

Without detailing the trials and tribulations that Shirak endures on what can only be described as his epic journey to reach Sinatra—only to be denied access at the end (91)—let it be said that the work is filled with, as the author himself characterizes them, "strange occurrences" and "acts of fate" (129–131). Like Odysseus's having to overcome, with strength and guile, one extraordinary obstacle after another on his journey home, so Shirak's attempts to capture the true essence of Sinatra/Hoboken involve extraordinary effort and patience.[12] From navigating the often-treacherous "proper channels" of Sinatra Enterprises (83) and conducting careful surveillance (80) to enduring three years of frustration and near misses (26, 90), Shirak's journey tests him and, by extension, all the people of Hoboken. His bid to honor Sinatra is best understood as an attempt to venerate that *genius Hobokenensis*, since his desire, first with the "From Here to Eternity" hotel, then "A Time That Was," and *Our Way* itself, bears a striking resemblance to the impulse that drove ancient Roman patricians to set up in their homes: "at first, wax-masks and, later, busts of their ancestors who had deserved well of their family or of the state . . . [as] a demonstration that they and all for which they stood still lived on and that they supplied the spiritual life to the family" (Barrow 20). Throughout his book, Shirak argues that, while Sinatra naturally deserves well for all for which he has stood, so, in fact, do the city and people of Hoboken. Ultimately, Frank, baseball, screw propeller steamboats, Stephen Foster, and all the uncelebrated men and women for whom Shirak speaks participate in the same spiritual life, the spirit of a town "whose courage and ideals stay with you" (126). (Indeed, all of New Jersey claims Sinatra as its own as seen in native sons' Bruce Springsteen and Jon Bon Jovi's very public declarations of his influence on them and their careers. Springsteen would open the Sinatra 80th birthday television salute in 1995, and Bon Jovi would lionize Sinatra's way in his 2000 song "It's My Life.")

"THERE ARE NO INNOCENT BYSTANDERS IN LAS VEGAS"

Although some things are similar in Hoboken and Las Vegas,[13] it is against a very different backdrop, and according to quite different standards of courage and ideals, that Michael Ventura depicts a comparable sense of the importance of heritage and place in his Vegas detective novel, *The Death of Frank Sinatra*. In the 1996 book, the reader follows a rather eventful few days in the life of private investigator Michael Rose (shortened from Rossellini), which begin with an attempt on his life and continue through a Sinatra concert and death scare, the demolition of the Dunes Casino by entrepreneur Steve Wynn, and his moblike murders of a close family friend and a client's husband. Thematically, however, the book centers on the historio-sociocultural significance of Las Vegas: from gambling and show biz to the Mafia and nuclear testing with Sinatra a defining element in the midst of it all.

Rose is a native Las Vegan and repeatedly refers to the way the city used to be: before the Steve Wynns of the world made it a family entertainment destination, before casinos became theme parks, before everyone wore the casually tacky clothes of tourists. He laments the loss of the era when even the parking attendants were casino professionals (Ventura 12) and describes a local establishment, Arizona Charlie's, as: "the kind of joint that used to be downtown and isn't anymore—an old-timey, rough-and-tumble gambling den" (21). Las Vegas is not the same town anymore, clearly a change for the worse. Even the landmarks of the Vegas landscape, from the Dunes Casino sign (116) to the "first topless joint" in the city (161), are in peril. Things are changing, and no one seems to care—nobody, that is, except Mike Rose, perhaps the sole legitimate heir of "old Vegas."

Despite a lifelong attempt to distance himself from his familial relationship to the mob (both dad and mom were part of the "Outfit"), Rose probably most embodies its ethos and the way things were: the respect and honesty with which colleagues treated one another and the sense of identity and place that came with those associations. In the mob, for example, the truest sign of one's impending death is being lied to (Ventura 26). Or, as he lamentingly suggests to one of his clients, Mrs. Sherman, about an etiquette that once existed in Vegas: "You don't ask questions about any action that doesn't involve you" (148). And action, as well as the etiquette that governs it, is quintessentially Vegas. Consequently, throughout the book, Rose ponders the various laws by which Vegas operates and the lessons it has taught him: "Scared money never wins" (15), "Never stop hitting a guy until he stops moving" (16), and "Stay in the action. Doesn't matter what that action is, as long as it's really yours" (106). The city is filled with such learning opportunities, but no one pays much attention to those lessons anymore.

In fact, it seems that, even in spite of himself, Mike Rose is especially sensitive to the meaning of Las Vegas. After a lifetime of consciously avoiding the footsteps of his hit man father, "Eddie Maybe,"—who was given his name for his penchant for always beginning his sentences with "maybe" (Ventura 30)—he apparently can never escape them fully. As he thinks at one particularly painful point, "sooner or later your heritage catches up to you, and either you survive that or you don't" (185). Even the tripartite organization of the novel, "Family," "Strangers," and "Ancestors," emphasizes the importance of this legacy.

What this brief but intense time in Rose's life comes to center upon, however, is a deeper understanding and appreciation of the meaning of this inheritance: from his mother's pornographic pictures to his father's murder by his lifelong friend, Isadore "Zig" Feldman, and whatever the mob knew about John Kennedy's assassination. For both Mike and his brother, Alvi, grappling with this complicated inheritance demands coming to terms with Frank Sinatra and his Vegas legacy.

On the most basic level, as has been well documented and as evidenced by Sinatra's authorship of the preface to Tom Campbell's 1984 book of photographs, *Las Vegas*, Sinatra and Vegas are inseparable because of the way he helped put the city on the entertainment map (Ventura 266). (It is no concidence that David and Don Was asked Frank Sinatra, Jr. to sing on their song "Wedding Vows in Vegas" on their 1988 album *What Up, Dog?*) It was Sinatra who as a headliner acted as a prime mover in "old Vegas," when it was an entertainment Mecca quite different from the sanitized, corporate atmosphere of the present-day strip. As a result, Sinatra serves for the narrator as a lens through which he can look back at both his own youth and that of Vegas itself. Thus, even obscure details of Sinatra's life link him directly to Vegas and Rose (224). In Rose's mind, for example, Sinatra's ownership of a company that built parts for guided missiles suggests that the singer owned something of the nuclear testing that long ago occurred outside Vegas (224–225) and helped to shape Rose into the man he is today—as the familial "metaphor" goes (96). Just as their parents believed Alvi's erratic character was shaped by his being born on a day it had snowed in Las Vegas, so Rose is the way he is (calculating yet explosive, loyal but decidedly independent) because he was born on the eve of a nuclear test in the nearby desert, back before the tests went underground (96). Not only would the explosion be the "first event he witnessed" (98), but subsequent tests would become occasions for festive pre-dawn Rossellini picnics to watch the blasts of light and pillars of smoke and to feel the shock waves and bursts of wind. While hindsight makes it clear that those blasts were most probably the cause of the thyroid cancer that would kill "Rosie Vee" two years ago at the age of sixty-five (99), as a memory of his youth (and the Vegas that he will never leave), they have a hold on Rose that he cannot—nor wants to—escape. In short, Sinatra plays a part in all that Vegas and Rose himself have been and are still, at least temporarily. As he watches the Dunes explode, for example, he feels the loss at his very core: "Rose's heart tore for the city he couldn't help but love—its neons that were, with the beauty of a few women, the only beauty he'd ever believed in, believed in helplessly, believed without wanting to, believed without believing, the way as a boy he'd believed in the grandeur of the bomb blasts" (238). The beauty and danger that Vegas explosions once possessed no longer applies. The contrived corporate nature of this staged detonation by Steve Wynn, in fact, only underscores how much Vegas has lost. "Grand" in only the safest of ways, the new city forces Rose to reap his most important lessons from the past.

On an even more personal level, Sinatra's significance comes from their mother's lifetime of admitting to a brief affair with the singer while she was a dancer at the Flamingo (Ventura 45), the first casino on the strip (72). Indeed, Rosie taunted Eddie by saying repeatedly that she married him because he resembled Sinatra when, in fact, his stockiness resembled Tony Bennett's physique far more than Frank's. That their two sons were Sinatra slender simply became a more disturbing part of the "tease" (45). Their mother also said that Mike, whose middle name is Francis, was named after Sinatra (120). Nevertheless, Rosie and Eddie loved each other in their own way. Despite having every one of Sinatra's recordings, for example, she never listened to them while her husband was in the house (219). Nor did she ever go to see Sinatra perform in Vegas either before or after Eddie was killed because, as Zig explains, "he woulda killed her. Even from the grave . . . And she *liked* him for that, respected that, *expected* that" (46). Clearly, for this private eye, complicated personal and professional relationships are what his family, Sinatra, and Vegas are all about. Indeed, so interconnected are they all that Rose can intuit, if not verbalize, that: "all their lives seemed mere expressions of the city" (69). And understanding those relationships necessitates thinking like his predecessors while still seeing both the past and present with "new eyes" (295).[14]

Thinking, acting, and seeing these relations anew are what eventually allow Mike Rose to survive and succeed. While he juggles clients like the WASPish Mrs. Sherman and avoids the mob threats to Alvi and himself, Rose is able to draw both on his intimate knowledge of the mob mind-set and his self-imposed distance from them to buy himself the time he needs finally to escape several attempts on his life.[15] As is the way with the detective fiction genre, although Rose knows far less than everyone else thinks he does (Ventura 9, 290–291), he plays the game better than they (89). Consciously having avoided the family business, for example, he always uses others' beliefs that he is "Mobbed up" to his advantage (95). He also can tell at a glance a well-trained hit man from a rookie and, when it becomes absolutely essential for his own survival, successfully can perform a hit himself.[16] Though this seemingly innate ability impresses his brother (262) and surprises and scares himself, Rose is a hybrid—taking the best of both the "Outfit" and "civilian" (85) worlds and creating a stronger and, yes, even better man.

He is, in a very real way, not the son of his father who, weak and afraid, was able neither to comfort his son nor to help him face up to his own fears. As Rose thinks about how he would alter the way Eddie Maybe used to look at him, he imagines his father: "put[ting] a hand on [my] shoulder, and show[ing me] a man's eyes that were not hard but were not afraid" (Ventura 296). For those were the only two types of eyes he ever saw from his father, Uncle Zig, and other associates: hard or afraid. As the novel proceeds, however, Rose's eyes are forced to see afresh. From coming to appreciate the significance—and strength—of the pornographic photographs of herself that his mother had left him (6) to his ability to avenge Zig's thirty-year-old murder of his father with his own comparably flawless execution in the desert (48–54), it is with a more complete knowledge and a resulting better appreciation of his past that Mike both survives and honors his ancestry.[17]

Of course, the problem with ancestral heritage is its inescapably complicated nature. Even the dead have something to say about most familial matters.[18] As Mike and Alvi learn firsthand: "the whole point of ancestors . . . is that they do give a shit" (Ventura 279). Everything about the past matters; the key is to make it work in one's favor . . . the way old-time mobsters like Meyer Lansky had done, the way their mother had done, the way Sinatra still does. For Frank, despite his age, still can smile a "smile that made him look uncannily young" (220) and can transmit "a kind of vitality that surged from the darkness with bright light" (222). And, as Rosie's "one indulgence of sentimentality" (223), her Sinatra scrapbook of pictures of the singer with an astoundingly diverse group of individuals, proved beyond a doubt that the: "body on the stage, that old man, was where it all connected" (224). Sinatra, through his personal connection to everyone from Carlo Gambino and Elvis Presley to Eleanor Roosevelt and Nancy Reagan (and particularly to Rosie Vee), thus intimately links them all to the Rossellini clan. Because of Sinatra's critical position, his death would sever irreparably those connections.

The title event of this 1996 novel, of course, is only a false alarm. Despite the rumors, Sinatra had not died; despite the endless tributes popping up on television and radio, he is still very much alive (Ventura 266). Nevertheless, as Mike had realized when he watched Sinatra leave the stage earlier in the evening, it would be only a matter a time. Although most fans do not realize it, the conclusions of his concerts are but rehearsals of his death (228). The inevitable is upon them all.

In the end, the book suggests that, even in 1996, Mike Rose and all of Las Vegas are experiencing the death of Frank Sinatra already. Sinatra's death, even if only metaphorically speaking, arrived the night of Sinatra's concert at the Desert Inn, the night Steve Wynn demolished the Dunes,[19] the night Mike killed Mr. Sherman so professionally, the night he refused to deal with Gino "The Touch" Lampedusa, the longtime head of the Vegas mob. His passing, however, is not merely a symbolic loss of innocence for the novel's characters; it is the final and irretrievable loss of old Vegas itself because with Rose's successful juggling of the Sherman case and his survival of Gino's threats comes, quite unintentionally, the rise to power of a junior member of the Outfit, Sallie Carlisi, a "monster" who remembers nothing of old Vegas (Ventura 299). Unlike the conventional hoods like "The Touch," Sallie is a cruel "pervert" who with real authority will try to change Vegas (299).[20] Thus, even though Sallie's ascendancy directly benefits the brothers Rossellini (e.g., they would not be killed and even obtain full ownership of Zig's old Vegas restaurant), it also clearly marks the end of Vegas as it had been. Sallie's complete ignorance of what the past holds (and, more significantly, his utter dismissal of its importance) stands in direct contrast to Mike's respect for its ways (289–290).[21]

As the book concludes with Mike and Alvi's watching the glow of the city in the west, the reader cannot but sense a finality to the past. Memories (of their parents, Zig, and the "situation" that initiated the whole course of events) are simply that: memories which, as such, lack the hold on the present and future that the living past of Vegas (and all it signified) once had. Despite any attempts the Rossellinis still might make to forestall it, yesterday, like Sinatra, is dead; the only thing for them to do now is cherish the memories, as troubling as they are, for as long as possible.

In the final analysis, both Shirak's and Ventura's books argue that the best anyone can do is try to preserve memories of Sinatra and his significance wherever possible. Chicago, for example, now has a street corner named Frank Sinatra Place. The New York Waterway trans-Hudson fleet boasts a ferry named after him, and a bronze statue of the singer is scheduled for Times Square in front of what had been the Paramount Theater. Las Vegas offers Frank Sinatra Drive as a north-south alternative to the Strip, while in Hoboken, Ed Shirak, Jr. continues to battle city leaders over his Sinatra museum. Plans for the Sinatra archives are even underway in Washington, D.C., as part of a national music museum. None of these monuments, of course, will ever compete with the man's own recorded performances, which will remain his most authentic and consequential contribution to cultural history. Nevertheless, with so many localities continuing to erect shrines in his honor, even Sinatra's physical place on the American landscape will be difficult to deny.

NOTES

1. For an interesting look at the changing view of cities in song, see B. Lee Cooper's *Images of American Society in Popular Music* (97–110).

2. With such songs as "Baltimore," "Birmingham," "Miami," and, of course, "Burn On" (his "tribute" to the fire on Cleveland's Cuyahoga River), among others, Randy Newman surely must be one of the most prolific of songwriters on the subject of individual cities. Nevertheless, those who know anything of his work will recognize immediately why most of his

sardonic songs have not endeared him to the residents of some cities in the same way "I Left My Heart in San Francisco" does to those in the Bay area.

3. In Don DeLillo's 1997 epic novel *Underworld*, Sinatra's presence at the October 3, 1951 playoff game between the Giants and the Dodgers places him at the very epicenter of New York mythology.

4. Sinatra tried to re-create the magic with "L.A. Is My Lady," but the song failed to catch on for little reason other than the Quincy Jones/Peggy Lipton/Carole Bayer Sager composition, not to mention its video, simply is not very good. Undoubtedly, it is the weakest cut on the 1984 Sinatra album that bears its title.

5. In some ways, given the author's ardent sense of reverent mission, a discussion of *Our Way* might have been included in the previous chapter instead.

6. Shirak and his business partner, Mario Lepore, published *Our Way* privately in Hoboken, a fact that the author understandingly declares quite proudly in the "Author's Note." Due to its private publication, however, the book bears many of the errors of an amateur author/publisher: not only a significant number of grammatical and syntactical errors, but also the misspelling of everything from the Latin of St. Peter "*Quo Vadis, Domine*" (2), to the names of radio host Sid Mark (2), singers Roy Orbison (18) and Bruce Springsteen (45), Charles Dickens's Madame Defarge (20), and comedian Tom—not Dan—Dreeson (86).

7. Mark's words become a refrain of sorts that challenges Shirak whenever the going gets tough (22, 92).

8. Sinatra also wore his Hoboken roots proudly, at least early on. At the beginning of his February 9, 1944, V-disc recording of "Long Ago and Far Away," for example, he introduces himself only as the "Hoodlum from Hoboken."

9. A similar distrust of lawyers (or anyone else who, in Shirak's opinion, discounts the "ordinary person") is also clear from his combative recounting of his Drunk While Intoxicated arrest and conviction (38–41).

10. As a writer, Shirak clearly prides himself on his sense of both the poetic and the symbolic and utilizes them throughout *Our Way*. The book titles he and Mario choose for Sinatra's chocolate presentation, for example—*A Tale of Two Cities* and *Oliver Twist*—are carefully considered (78), as is his enumeration of the "points" that make Sinatra the brightest star in the entertainment firmament, "whether it be the star of David having six points or the star of Bethlehem with 5 points" (116–117).

11. This personal dimension cannot be emphasized too much since it underscores the communal nature of Shirak's book. The text even includes messages for Frank from Hoboken residents. For example, concerning a house purchased thirty years ago from Marty and Dolly Sinatra, Vince and Mary Giusto want: "Mr. Sinatra to know that the house [in Weehawken, N.J.] is

still maintained in the same immaculate order, the same way it was left to them by his parents" (Shirak 120).

12. Homer's *Odyssey*, as Norman Austin argues, is, in the final analysis, about *homophrosyne*, that is, the "like-mindedness" which the hero shares with Penelope (181), and this intimate bond to Ithaca, his home, keeps Odysseus alive, drives all of his actions, and even compels him to reject the promise of immortality offered by Calypso.

13. Like Ed Shirak, Jr., the private detective, Mike Rose, repeatedly must face people who dismiss him as "nothing" (60).

14. A variety of eyes dominate the final chapters of the novel: Mike's eyes as they feel the Dunes blast (239), Gino's that are utterly empty (290), and, of course, Sinatra's that are preternaturally youthful (221).

15. As Alvi introduces his brother to boast of his toughness: "He calls himself Mike Rose. That's 'cause he hates his ancestors. He hates everybody. He hates you" (277).

16. This same sense of toughness is what the "emo" band The Jazz June try to capture in its 2000 song, "Fight like Sinatra."

17. He comes to see the nude photographs of his mother as the portraits of a woman who "was out to prove something to herself," and was successful in her attempt; consequently, "his respect for his father grew" (285).

18. A subplot of the novel is Alvi's interest in converting to Mormonism, in which one is saved along with one's entire family, living and deceased. Alvi's need to research his family tree gets Zig quite nervous concerning what he might uncover about his family's involvement in the actions of the "Outfit," the very information that got their father killed thirty years before.

19. Fittingly, in April 2000, Steve Wynn bought and, on August 28, closed the half-century-old Desert Inn on the Strip to replace it with another new resort hotel.

20. The spiritual advisor/madam, Reverend Joy, tells Mike, for example, of Sallie's decades-old habit of hiring a prostitute on his birthday, having his way with her, and killing her, before returning to his family (299).

21. His first act as owner of the restaurant will be the removal of all the video poker games that he feels destroy its ambiance as the only true Vegas bar (305).

CHAPTER **11**

"Gonna Sit Right Down and Write Myself a Letter": Blaming the Oyster in *Sinatraland*

In "Oyster Shucker," the premier episode of Sinatra's often self-referential 1953–1954 radio series, *Rocky Fortune*, the "footloose and fancy free" title character stumbles upon an oyster smuggling ring fronted by a seafood restaurant. After surviving several threats upon his life, he finds himself in legal possession of a dozen pearls, not to mention in the company of Iris, the lovely restaurant cashier. As the radio series would illustrate weekly, however, no good luck ever accompanies Rocky for long. Iris, in fact, is an undercover officer and, even as he gives her the pearls as a token of his affection, she issues him a "property receipt" from U.S. Customs. From windfall to tax debt in the blink of two lovely eyes: such is Rocky's fortune!

An even more complex examination of the price of pearls is at the heart of Sam Kashner's 1999 epistolary novel, *Sinatraland*.[1] In the final letter that "Finkie" Finklestein writes to Frank Sinatra just after the singer's death in May 1998, the window-blind-salesman-turned-member-of-the-Sinatra-inner-circle finally confesses how much he has given up for Sinatraland, especially his first wife and daughter (Kashner 192). He nonetheless accepts: "the blame for all that living in Sinatraland has brought down on the House of Finklestein, the way that an oyster has to accept blame for the pearl" (192).

And so it goes. Even as he ultimately seems to face up to the high cost of his lifetime obsession with the "chairman of the board," Finkie cannot but view it as a process that has produced something valuable, something precious, something that could have been created in no other way. Even as he sees the value of his own life slipping away (to which his angry outburst toward his deceased idol at the beginning of the letter clearly attests), he cannot help but consider all the pain, both psychic and physical, well worth his while. Just as an oyster can produce a pearl only when a foreign object gets under its skin, as it were, so his appreciation of Sinatra has grown due, in large part, to its own series of irritations. He has endured much during his lifetime of Sinatra-watching (stalking?). He has withstood everything from the minor and imaginary trials—his not being able to share Frank's pain after the singer's license to run the Cal-Neva Lodge and Casino is revoked by the "G-men" (Kashner 31–33) and Frank's not coming to his financial aid for medical expenses when he passed out from low blood sugar at Disneyland (44)—to the major and decidedly personal—his being a suspect in a murder and the life-threatening beating he receives from Sinatra's security guards following his retirement concert (169–170).[2] In short, every "close call" that Finkie and Frank would share throughout the years (even when they were merely fanciful) only added another layer to this gem of a one-sided relationship.

By the time Finkie is invited to join Sinatra's inner circle (a clearly preemptive move by Sinatra's people against possible litigation for the assault on Finklestein after the 1971 concert), Finkie has risen and fallen many times with his dear friend, Francis. He trumpets the singer's patriotism, evidenced by Frank's achievement of performing in a pair of presidential assassination films (Kashner 73); he vows to never play a Sinatra record again until Frank, Jr. is released by his kidnappers in 1963 (24); nor does he leave his house until Frederick Weisman comes out of his coma, the result of a well-publicized scuffle with Sinatra (123). Thanks to Finkie's lifelong fascination with Sinatra, the two men, it would seem, share far more than their Hoboken roots.

Not surprisingly, much of what Finklestein and Sinatra share is only wishful thinking on the narrator's part. His first "close call" with Frank, for example, is how he could have been at the Imperial Gardens restaurant on the night he later learned the singer reportedly proposed to Lauren Bacall, who had been widowed by Humphrey Bogart only the year before.[3] Finkie, who was in the area on a business trip, unfortu-

nately had to turn down a friend's dinner invitation because he was ill
(Kashner 10). Both Frank and Finkie are romantic nonetheless (10):
Frank proposes rather impetuously to Bogie's widow, and Finkie once
dedicated a song to his "future ex-girlfriend" (11)—two quite comparable events to any objective observer! The wedding gift he and first
wife Jill receive from her father, a yacht club membership, makes him
feel like Sinatra in *Pal Joey* (74). In addition, he fancies his friends similar to Sinatra's famous cronies. Fellow Weiss and Rifkind employee Milton Fine is his Jilly Rizzo (25), and, for a while, he even formed his own
Rat Pack with three coworkers and their version of Sammy Davis, Jr.,
his maid's husband (34). Nor does either of them necessarily appreciate
the limits of joking. Frank, as his biographers commonly report, was
fired from MGM for making a joke about Louis B. Mayer and his
"companion" Ginny Simms (Taraborrelli 110), while Finkie misses the
opportunity for a major career advancement by setting off cherry
bombs in the shoes of his interviewer (Kashner 34).

This forced parallelism by Finkie is, of course, a large part of author
Kashner's point. Finkie is a Sinatra-wannabe without the talent, one of
the "weeping slobs" to whom Sinatra gave a voice (Kashner 161). When
Finkie begins to lose his nerve about seeing Frank in person at his retirement concert, for example, his wife, Odette, encourages him by
pointing out that the moment had arrived "to face yourself" (167).
Finkie always has seen himself in Sinatra. Now, Odette hopes that he finally will view himself as a unique individual, one distinct and free from
Sinatra. Finkie, however, never does. He never abandons his Sinatraland
completely. Sinatra and he remain bound inextricably, and their ultimate bond is their loneliness.

Kashner's novel consists of a series of thirty-five letters divided un-
equally into five chapters, each named after a Sinatra song and each with
a particular but not exclusive emphasis. "Love and Marriage" (fifteen
letters), for example, extending from the late 1950s to the early1960s,
introduces readers to Jill, his first wife, and his only child, Nancy Ava.
The letters of "Glad to Be Unhappy" (eight letters) discuss mostly the
mid-1960s and recount his affair with Rosalie Haines, while "Strangers
in the Night" (seven letters) concludes the 1960s and relates the murder
of Rosalie and its aftermath. In "The Second Time Around" (three letters), readers meet Odette, Finkie's second wife, and learn of the trau-
matic events of Sinatra's retirement concert. Finally, "Everything
Happens to Me" (two letters) covers Finkie's life amidst the Sinatra reti-
nue, from 1971 to Sinatra's death in 1998. The first letter of this final
section, to Jill who has remarried and moved to Michigan, is the only

letter not addressed to Sinatra, while the final letter of the book serves as
Finkie's rather emotional farewell to the recently deceased entertainer.
Interspersed throughout the chapters, however, are the stories of a variety of characters, including Finkie's daughter, his brother, Myron, and
his Uncle Dave, not to mention briefer stories of friends and colleagues,
as well as personalities and celebrities both major and minor.

A jumble of anecdote, confession, and gossip, the letters never stray
too far from Frank's latest album, film, or relationship, even as they relate Finkie's own personal and professional struggles. As much as Finkie
thinks he is living a richly fulfilling existence, his emphasis upon Sinatra's family, friends, and acquaintances only exposes his quest to understand himself almost solely through the life and times of his favorite
singer. It also becomes clear that, for all the activity in both men's lives,
there seems to be an inescapable emptiness at their centers.

Kashner, after the release of *Sinatraland*, published a profile of Sinatra in *Gentleman's Quarterly*, entitled "The Loneliest Guy in the
World," which cannot be read as anything but a gloss on his novel. The
emphases of the novel and article are similar, and aspects of Sinatra's biography, not to mention characteristics of Sinatra's personality, are ever
at play in both pieces. The two men, Finkie and Frank, for example, are
contemporaries, hail from Hoboken (*Sinatraland* 181), and attended
the same high school (126–127). They both face the issues of growing
older in an America that from the mid-1950s on is increasingly dominated by the young. Just as Frank "simply didn't get" the protest movements of the 1960s ("Loneliest" 358), so Finkie is puzzled by daughter
Nancy Ava's activism (146–147). During the investigation of the murder of Finkie's girlfriend, Rosalie Haines, the tabloids refer to him as an
"aging swinger" (142), the very same phrase that Kashner uses to de-
scribe the Sinatra of the *Tony Rome* period ("Loneliest" 356). Finkie's
beating at the hands of Sinatra's security detail is reminiscent of the
mob's brutality toward comedian Shecky Greene due to some disre-
spect he had shown the singer ("Loneliest" 356). The coldness of the
relationship between Frank, Jr. and his father is something that Finkie
criticizes in his final letter (*Sinatraland* 190–191) and that Kashner underscores in his profile ("Loneliest" 344). Sinatra's "yearning for class"
("Loneliest" 352) is mirrored in Finkie's complicated relationship with
Jill's family, the Bronsteins (*Sinatraland* 74–75).

As Kashner emphasizes, Finkie is not well educated. His prose attempts, if not erudition, then a kind of urbanity—but falls far short. The
text, for example, is sprinkled with malapropisms: his fear of becoming a
"persona au gratin" (*Sinatraland* 55); the "optimum illusion" of re-

uniting with Jill, his first wife (73); not to mention all the names of women who shall remain "amphibious" (122).[4] He is prone to mixed metaphor, less-than-felicitous expression, and twisted logic, as well. He writes of how Jill "put her foot down with a strong hand" (18), how his daughter was named after Frank's "first two successful marriages" (19), and how, unlike Frank, who had been too emotional to attend the funeral of Mocambo owner Charlie Morrison, Finkie attended "since he didn't know him well enough to be that broken up" (46).

Nor is Finkie's taste, even regarding Sinatra, above reproach. He boasts that Frank and Tony Curtis are his two favorite painters (51), declares *Ocean's 11* a "masterpiece" (37), and readily admits that he never would have read another book if not for all the waiting during his second wife Odette's hysterectomy (162).

In many ways, therefore, his formal education is comparable to Frank's, who, as it is well known, dropped out of Demarest High School in Hoboken in his senior year (Nancy Sinatra 20). But whereas Sinatra never stopped learning and utilized his fame to seek out, among others, Bennett Cerf (*Sinatraland* 62)—or as Sinatra referred to him, "the bookmaker" (Kashner, "Loneliest" 352)—Finkie learns the correct way to spell W.H. Auden's name from stripper Gypsy Rose Lee on a snowy night in Chicago (*Sinatraland* 70) and listens to Carl Sandburg records with actress/unsolved murder victim, Karyn Kupcinet (36). Finkie, in short, does not try too hard to better himself, despite a little night school (31) and whatever Odette manages to teach him (186–187), but assumes that he remains as sophisticated as Sinatra nevertheless. Mr. Sinatra, after all, would be the first to recognize that Finkie's play about the kidnapping of Frank, Jr. is not exploitative, and the people who reject it simply do not share their refinement (27), for Finkie and Frank share a bond more intimate than even brothers; they share Sinatraland.

While many, including our narrator, have uttered the oft-quoted aphorism "It's Frank's world, we only live in it" (*Sinatraland* 76–77), to Finkie's mind, he and Frank are the only two permanent residents of this Sinatraland: a place in which everything bears the stamp of its creator, Frank Sinatra. That, of course, is why the short-lived Cal-Neva represents to Finkie "Sinatraland writ large" because of how it: "reflected your ideas, even your favorite colors . . . how every detail . . . was hand picked by Frank Sinatra himself" (31). Cal-Neva was a combination of New Jersey, Las Vegas, and Palm Springs (31), and, as Finkie so succinctly and devoutly puts it: "God, we were happy there" (32).

With its unfortunate demise at the hands of the gaming commission, Cal-Neva takes on a significance for Finkie that cannot be overstated, for it embodied Sinatra in a way no other place could. It epitomized Sinatra's past even as it clearly pointed to his future, which is why, for Finkie, at least, it was probably best that it did not survive. The Sinatraland of Finkie Finklestein, of necessity, exists in a world apart. It exists independently of the responsibilities governed by what other mortals term "time and space."

Indeed, Finkie tries his best to live according to his own clock, as seen by the importance placed upon the gift of timepieces throughout the novel. For example, there is the wristwatch Jill gave him on their "tenth and last" anniversary (*Sinatraland* 43), the bar mitzvah watch that his mother never gave him but which he would discover after her death (187), and the watch Sinatra had given to his new employee, which the singer in a fit of anger later threw into a sand trap (183). But the most significant timepiece of all, as well as the clearest proof that Sinatraland is, in the end, neither a particular time or place but rather a state of mind, was Finklestein's "internal Sinatra clock," a way of reckoning time according to the singer's "stage time" (42). And this is what separates Finkie from everybody else. As he puts it most aptly, he is especially lucky to have Sinatra "not in the brain, but the chest" (42). Even as he is drawn by his various relationships, he still reckons his life primarily in accordance with Sinatra. Sinatra (and not his wife, mother, or daughter) is with whom he shares his heart.

Despite all these different timepieces (and maybe even because of them), Finkie is forever out of sync with the other people in his life. When he considers the time his marriage to Jill began to crumble, he comments on how his "timing was off." When she would be interested in a night on the town, he would be anticipating "loosening my belt and watching Archie Moore fight on television" (*Sinatraland* 133). In fact, as he writes in the letter immediately following his beating, the bad timing and the discord of family and friends that living in Sinatraland facilitates is at the core of Sinatraland; it is a: "dream in which nothing was real but the waiting, whether it was for night to come or waiting for the women for whom we cause so much pain" (168). Such a continuous state of inaction cannot but hurt the relationships a man has with flesh-and-blood people as close as wives and daughters. Nevertheless, when the invitation to join Sinatra's inner circle comes, much to second wife Odette's disbelief, he accepts (180). He willingly risks a happy marriage to a smart and understanding woman to join the very entourage that nearly killed him, just as he, in effect, had chosen Sinatra over both Jill, his first wife and one true love (185), and his daughter.

Throughout the letters, Finkie (unknowingly, at first) documents his family's alienation from himself due to his residency in Sinatraland. Jill is no longer happy there after a while (Kashner, *Sinatraland* 133); Odette argues that he intentionally has missed Sinatra throughout the years because finally facing Sinatra would make it all the more difficult to pretend that they shared anything in common (165). Nevertheless, at that very concert, the moment Sinatra starts singing, the narrator eagerly welcomes Jill, Nancy Ava, and Rosalie back into Sinatraland. They all are present once again, and "I had no quarrel with the past. I just listened, helpless, as you dropped the net of my life over me" (167–168). The net of his life ensnares everyone close to him, whether they like it or not. And no matter how many people are in his life, he is—like the Sinatra of Kashner's *GQ* profile—alone, whether he knows it or not.

While fascinating in themselves as a psychological portrait of a fan(atic), the obsessive details of *Sinatraland* raise the real question of the novel: what is the source of this shared loneliness? While it is clear that the singer means the world to him, readers can never be sure what precisely Finkie's world is. Of course, it is populated with a variety of colorful characters (everyone from show people and the family Finklestein to shade salesmen and the Kennedys); nevertheless, they all clearly take a backseat in Finkie's mind to Sinatra. Readers need to see if and how all these lines can be shown to intersect, independent of Finkie's own twisted perspective. That crossroads comes in the person of Uncle Dave Finklestein.

In Uncle Dave, the author has provided readers with a prism through which Sinatra's status as celebrity, commodity, and private obsession can be viewed and evaluated. Finkie's Uncle Dave is a Russian immigrant who managed to parley his expertise with the bullwhip into a brief stint in silent films. He, however, quickly loses his movie career, if that is even the appropriate description of it, when the talking film is developed and his heavy Jewish accent makes speaking parts highly improbable. Nonetheless, having "convinced himself he was an important man" (Kashner, *Sinatraland* 116), Dave spends the rest of his life as a marginal informant who would sell a few "items" to New York columnists, such as Walter Winchell and Earl Wilson (110–111).[5] Dave, however, for all his determination, could also be his own worst enemy. He lost one of his most promising job opportunities when he made an ill-advised joke, similar to Sinatra's about Louis B. Mayer, directed at *My Fair Lady* playwright lyricist, Alan Jay Lerner (111–112). In Uncle

Dave, Kashner thus offers another Finklestein who is not only a comparably deluded individual, but also one who even is willing to go to great lengths for the privilege of only seeming to be included. Uncle Dave, despite his longevity on the Great White Way (even according to his loving nephew), had no friends, no talent, and no real success at any level (116). He simply refused to leave and, in the end, was "as stage-struck as a little girl" (116).

Despite how it may appear, in both Finkie and Uncle Dave, Kashner is not simply attacking these archetypal fans' need to "get a life." Uncle Dave had a life (and a terribly exciting story to tell), if he had only wanted to tell it. As Finkie suggests, what Dave should have been talking about was the very thing he refused to discuss: his life in the old country in the Tsar's army (117). Instead, as he aged, he only dreamt of retiring to Arizona to write his show business memoirs!

The parallels are clear. What if Finkie himself had stopped writing letters that Sinatra never answered; stopped living his life according to his "internal Sinatra clock"; stopped living in Sinatraland altogether and focused on his wife, daughter, family, and friends instead? Would not that have been a life lived fully? Would not that have been a life worth writing and reading about? Instead, by the time he hooks up with Sinatra and enters Sinatraland proper, Frank himself has become an "egghead" who lives quietly in the desert, painting, reading, and playing with his model trains (Kashner, *Sinatraland* 185). Consequently, Finkie has wasted his life in waiting for a chance at an existence that, when he finally wins it, no longer exists. Sinatraland may have opened once again (179), but its familiar landscape has been altered radically. All that waiting had been essentially for naught.

Of course, as the years go by and Finkie occasionally seems on the verge of finally changing, of finally discovering the internal void that Sinatraland has hid from him,[6] he always falls back upon the power with which Frank seemingly grants him. As he confesses to Jill, he owes Sinatra for how he had accompanied him and "made [him] feel potent" through even the toughest times in his life—as a travelling salesman, during his divorce from Jill, and especially when his thoughts turned to the murdered Rosalie: "which was usually whenever I thought about how much effort goes into being alive." (178). At those points, Finkie speaks of how he would hear Sinatra and: "imagine him putting on his raincoat and stepping out with me into the unknown future" (178). His notion of potency, of course, underscores his real problem. While imagining Frank's striking that archetypal *Pal Joey* pose with a raincoat and fedora, Finkie does not see the way things are, the actual amount of effort it takes to survive. It can be argued, in fact, that, forever blinded (or, at the very least, dazzled) by Sinatra's jauntily titled hat, Finkie cannot appreciate life sufficiently. Instead, he simply must pretend to understand its pain.[7]

Finkie's emotional displays must be pretense because readers are hard pressed to accept the notion that Finkie truly has experienced what he tries to explain to brother Myron about the "pain of pain" (109), which Finkie describes as being kicked out of one's home and gassing up the car: "to go God knows where, and you kick the front tire so hard that you practically break your foot so that now you can really howl at the moon and bring tears to your eyes" (109). While one can conceive of Jill's throwing him out of the house as their marriage crumbles, one can only see such a scene as he describes as a childish or hackneyed pantomime. It is melodramatic and does not ring true.[8]

To Finkie, his brother may be someone who has never been close to another person (109), but Finkie is the guy who never fully has invested in any relationship other than the one he shares with Frank. He continued to live with his brother, for example, *even after he secretly had been married to Jill for several years* (21), yet he characterizes the time during which Frank, Jr. was held by kidnappers as "the worst fifty-four hours" of his life (24). He clearly is a man who has isolated himself in a dream world all his own, something he shares only with his idol.

As former Sinatra publicist Peter Levinson tells Kashner about Sinatra: "Even though he had that whole 'come fly with me' reputation . . . I never thought Frank ever felt at home in the world. The nightclub floor, the concert stage, those were the only places he felt at home. To me, this great artist was a lost soul." (Kashner "Loneliest" 358). And Finkie is equally and irretrievably lost. He is never alone in his life, but, at the same time, he is never completely there for his family and friends. Even after Sinatra's death when he chooses to leave Sinatraland, he suggests his decision is based upon the fear of losing his family permanently (Kashner, *Sinatraland* 192). Nevertheless, having left Sinatra's service and concluding his correspondence with the deceased singer, he does not abandon fully his relationship with Sinatra since he leaves open the possibility—and even necessity—of further contact in his humorous (but somehow credible) postscript: "P.S. If you screw Jill up there I'll never talk to you again" (192).

Some may argue to the contrary: that the final sentence of the body of the letter suggests growth and maturation, not stagnation or stasis. After all, in it he finally seems to acknowledge both the human cost that everyone has paid ("the world is filling up with the dead") as well as the

wasted time (192). Unfortunately, according to his P.S., his true resi-
dence, Sinatraland—that world where every woman is a "mouse" who
cannot but find Frank irresistible—extends to the next world. Finkie
may still be on earth, but the promise of an afterlife with Frank (a celes-
tial Cal-Neva?) awaits him.

Readers must remember that Finkie accepts the blame for everything, "the way an oyster has to accept the blame for the pearl" (192).
The gem that is Finkie's life may not be perfect, but it is entirely his own
in a way that not even his daughter is. Unlike Nancy Ava, who had both
Finkie and Jill as her parents, Sinatraland is entirely of his own creation,
a product of his mind alone. Just as Zeus always possesses a special bond
with Athena, the daughter born from his own forehead, so Sinatraland
will always hold an uncontested place in Finkie's heart. His solitary act
of generation, like the oyster's formation of a pearl, holds a value for
him that is uniquely precious. And while such an affinity may never
keep Finkie warm at night, it possesses an immanence unapproached in
any of his other relationships.[9]

Finkie is, in the end, to blame for Sinatraland just as Sinatra, finally, is
to blame for his voice. Its price may be very high for both men, but, for
Finkie, ah, what a voice—and, ah, what a place!

NOTES

1. The epistolary nature of the novel recalls the form of the foreward that
Sinatra contributed to *The Big Bands* by George T. Simon. Sinatra's "letter,"
supposedly penned in reply to "Joe Oakes" of "1234 Oak Street, Middletown,
USA," offers the 1967 book as the "definitive" answer to all of Joe's questions (Simon vii–x).

2. Sinatra, in fact, does send money to Finkie when he loses his job after
the Weiss and Rifkind window shade business closes due to the collapse of
the roof (Kashner, *Sinatraland* 16). He, of course, cannot understand why
the check is not drawn on Sinatra's personal account but rather from a Sands
Hotel account, and signed by Jack Entratter, the manager of the Las Vegas
casino (16). Remarkably, this was not even the first time he had asked Sinatra
for money. Boldly equating himself with others whom Sinatra had helped
with medical expenses—Lee J. Cobb and Bela Lugosi (47), for example—
Finkie first had sought financial assistance from Sinatra after his Disneyland
collapse (44).

3. In a comedy sketch from a 1945 episode of *Command Performance*, a
radio series aired especially for members of the armed forces during and after
World War II, Bogart turns to Frank to serve as bodyguard for Bacall only to
lose her to the singer. The plot, inspired by a soldier's request for a program
based upon the outlandishly comic premise that Bogart could lose Bacall to

Sinatra, underscores how much Sinatra's image had changed between Frank's early fame and his post-comeback rise. When Sinatra proposes to Bacall in 1958, a year after Bogart's death, he is no longer the skinny lad who only is of interest to thirteen-year-old girls. He is the legitimate heir of the Rat Pack of Bogart, Bacall, Judy Garland, Sid Luft, Swifty Lazar, David and Hjordis Niven, and Mike and Gloria Romanoff. As William Modic argued in a paper delivered at the 1996 conference of the Northeast Popular Culture Association, besides reflecting the decidedly different character of its new leader, Sinatra's version of the Rat Pack, "The Clan," also reflected the change that Hollywood itself had undergone with the weakening of the studio system and the rise of independently powerful actors and agents.

4. He even manages to confuse the classic Rat Pack nickname for Kennedy in-law Peter Lawford, the "brother-in-Lawford." Finkie's version is the redundant "Lawford-in-Law" (Kashner, *Sinataland* 20).

5. A professional and personal supporter of Sinatra (Freedland 225), Walter Winchell nevertheless would pass on to the FBI "a reader's letter asserting that the FBI was investigating whether the singer had bribed his way out of the draft." In fact, the bureau had not been "investigating any such thing, the tip insured it did" (Kuntz and Kuntz xv). Columnist Earl Wilson, as he writes in the preface of his biography of the entertainer, after "more than a quarter of a century" of being his "friend, booster, and most consistent defender among the columnists," was barred from Sinatra shows because, according to a publicist, he had written "something [Sinatra] didn't like" (Wilson ix).

6. In the second chapter, for example, Finkie confesses to Frank his own and every other man's ultimate insecurity—every man, that is, except Frank (Kashner, *Sinataland* 76). And in the penultimate letter, he asks Jill not to feel sorry for him because he is no longer as resistant to change as she once thought him to be (185).

7. Finkie's artificiality perhaps could be the reason why students in English 288, "The Literary Sinatra" class at Central Connecticut State University, have tended to read (incorrectly, in my view) the hat and raincoat that appear on the hat rack in Finkie's hospital room not as Sinatra's at all. Rather, they argue that it probably is a morale-boosting deception played upon the ailing Finkie by Myron or Odette.

8. Due to its reliance on hip "Sinatraspeak," Finkie's "philosophy of tears" shares the same hollow ring (Kashner, *Sinatraland* 51).

9. Finkie's recitation of Sinatra's autobiographical story of the hero, gifted with a remarkable voice, who wants to fill his house with life, makes the same point (Kashner, *Sinatraland* 183–184). While the voice can do marvelous things, it cannot make the house any warmer, brighter, or livelier (184). It may be able to "give hope to us humans" (90), but ultimately it cannot save the singer from his own feeling of isolation.

Sinatriad: The Unwritten American Epic

Sing, muses, sing of Sinatra, the voice that sang America . . .

With Frank Sinatra's death of a heart attack on Thursday, May 14, 1998, came the official end of the twentieth century (Hemming and Hajdu 117). Now the time has come to consider a worthy memorial. As a specialist in Neo-Latin literature, I humbly would suggest a *Sinatriad*, a traditional epic poem about the preeminent icon of this American century. Nothing less would do Sinatra justice. A miniseries, documentary, or Hollywood biopic simply cannot possess the intensity, weight, and scope that were Sinatra's life and work. On the other hand, an epic— a long narrative poem of national significance recounting the remarkable deeds of a decidedly human champion—fits the bill precisely. It is a shame that epics have fallen out of fashion, otherwise the next Homer, Vergil, or Milton undoubtedly would be invoking the muse and polishing his verses.

The life and career of Sinatra embody the vast cultural and political changes in America since his birth in 1915. Beginning in working-class Hoboken, the singer's odyssey spans the twentieth-century American landscape: from the technicolor Hollywood of the 1940s through neon-lighted Las Vegas and the promise of JFK's Camelot to the rise of Reaganism in the 1980s and beyond.

Indeed, for sixty years, Sinatra epitomized America's many moods and directions as no one else could or did. His wartime musicals, in which he always seemed to portray a sailor, exude an innocent confidence in America's ability to save the world. His dedication to FDR's liberalism, exemplified by his 1945 Oscar-winning short *The House I Live In* (not to mention the naming of Frank, Jr. after Franklin D., not Francis A.), led him later to support blacklisted Hollywood writers and make such socially perceptive films as *Suddenly, Kings Go Forth, The Manchurian Candidate*, and *None but the Brave*. His association with John F. Kennedy only added to the romantic glamour of the early 1960s. But, by the early 1970s, the triumph of youth culture forced Sinatra into premature retirement, only to return a conservative elder statesman doing it his way and performing to sold-out audiences through the mid-1990s.

Sinatra's private life was never very private, with the famous women always on his arm, the underworld figures very occasionally at his side, and the Soviet Premier, Nikita Khrushchev, on his movie set. His hard-living, often combative, personality regularly made headlines for punching photographers, feuding with gaming commissions, and battling Australia. (What could be more epic than provoking an entire continent!?)

Even with the larger-than-life characters who would fill the *Sinatriad* (Crosby, Dorsey, Riddle, Davis, Martin, Basie, MacLaine, et al.), it is Sinatra's quartet of wives who merit special epic attention. They mirrored the changing currents of not only this American hero, but also our culture. First, there was Nancy Barbato, his childhood sweetheart and mother of his children, who, since their divorce in 1951, never has spoken out publicly against him. Ava Gardner—actress, other woman, and soul mate—was as passionate and volatile as Sinatra, so they were no happier living together than apart. His short-lived marriage in the mid-1960s to Mia Farrow clearly manifested Sinatra's tortured attempts to conquer the youth market. Finally, Barbara Marx, Frank's longtime and devoted partner, has successfully employed the Sinatra name for a multitude of important charitable causes. Like Helen of Troy or Dido, these women crystallize the conflicted picture of Sinatra as spouse and cad, romantic and rake.

Of course, the *Sinatriad* will never be written because it would be redundant. This heroic song, inspired by the muses and recounting the glories and tragedies of a remarkable man, already exists in Sinatra's musical legacy. His victories and losses, as well as his strengths and flaws, are captured in every song Frank ever sang: the purity of "This Love of Mine," the heartache of "I'm a Fool to Want You," the swagger of "I've Got the World on a String," the fragility of "In the Wee Small Hours of the Morning," and, yes, the pomposity of "My Way" and "New York, New York."

Epic, after all, is not hagiography, and epic heroes are not role models. The great epics, such as the *Iliad*, *Aeneid*, and *Paradise Lost*, succeed because they recognize both the sublime and baser natures of humanity. Sinatra was no saint, even if his singing was heaven-sent, and, through his epic song, Frank Sinatra, for better or worse, gave America its voice.

APPENDIX I

A Chronological Listing of Frank Sinatra's Reprise Albums for Which Stan Cornyn Wrote the Liner Notes

1964 *It Might as Well Be Swing* (interview with Quincy Jones, arranger/conductor)

Softly as I Leave You

1965 *Sinatra '65* (interview with Jimmy Bowen, producer)

*September of My Years**#*

My Kind of Broadway (interview with Sonny Burke, producer)

Sinatra: A Man and His Music

1966 *Strangers in the Night*

Moonlight Sinatra

*Sinatra at the Sands**#*

That's Life

1967 *Francis Albert Sinatra and Antonio Carlos Jobim**

Frank Sinatra: The World We Knew

1968 *Francis A. and Edward K.**

1969 *My Way*

1973 *Ol' Blue Eyes Is Back* *

1984 *L.A. Is My Lady*

1995 *Frank Sinatra: The Complete Reprise Studio Recordings*

*Grammy Nomination for Best Album Notes (Annotator's Award)
#Grammy Winner for Best Album Notes (Annotator's Award)

APPENDIX II

A Chronological Listing of Original Songs Mentioning Frank Sinatra (Selected)

Title	Artist	Date
	1940s	
"Gotta Be This or That"	Benny Goodman	1945
"I'd Rather Be with You"	Les Brown (with Doris Day and Johnny Parker)	1945
"I Want a Grown Up Man"	Anita O'Day	1945
"Jumpin' at the Record Shop"	Slim Gaillard	1945
"Bobby Sox Blues"	T-Bone Walker	1946
"So Round, So Firm, So Fully Packed"	Merle Travis	1947
"Put 'em in a Box, Tie 'em with a Ribbon, and Throw 'em in the Deep Blue Sea"	Doris Day	1948
	1960s	
"Bachelor in Paradise"	Henry Mancini	1961
"It's a Breeze"	Matt Monro	1964
"New Age"	Velvet Underground	1969
	1970s	
"Hard Nose the Highway"	Van Morrison	1973
"On and On"	Stephen Bishop	1976

Title	Artist	Date
"It's Over Now"	Beach Boys	1977
"Headlines"	Paul Anka	1979

1980s

"We Love You"	The Psychedelic Furs	1980
"Pirates (So Long Lonely Avenue)"	Rickie Lee Jones	1981
"Sinatra Serenade"	Art in America	1983
"Deportees Club"	Elvis Costello and the	
	Attractions	1984
"That's America"	Johnny Taylor	1984
"Life in a Northern Town"	Dream Academy	1985
"Sugar Mice"	Marillion	1987
"More than Sinatra"	Jane Ira Bloom	1987
"Fairytale of New York"	The Pogues (with	
	Kirsty McColl)	1988
"Hey Manhattan"	Prefab Sprout	1988

1990s

"Where Did the Magic Go?"	Tony Bennett	1990
"She Goes On"	Crowded House	1991
"Sinatra"	Helmet	1992
"Teen Angst (What the World Needs Now)"	Cracker	1992
"T.S.M.N.W.A."	Loudon Wainwright III	1993
"If I Were Frank Sinatra"	Soulvitamins	1993
"September Skies"	The Brian Setzer Orchestra	1994
"Hang Sinatra"	Natasha's Ghost	1995
"Sinatra Mantra"	Victim's Family	1995
"Frank Sinatra"	Benett	1996
"Frank Sinatra"	Cake	1996
"The Sound of North America"	The Beautiful South	1996
"Padrino"	Smash Mouth	1997
"Sammy	GWAR	1997
"Here's to the Man"	Barry Manilow	1998
"One Man in a Spotlight"	Barry Manilow	1998
"Some Sinatra"	Secret Stars	1998
"Sinatra's Dead"	Mannix	1999

2000

"Sinatra"	Big Fish Ensemble	2000
"It's My Life"	Bon Jovi	2000
"(Not a) Dank Sinatra"	DJ Eddie Def	2000
"Fight Like Sinatra"	The Jazz June	2000
"Frank Sinatra"	Michael Veitch	2000
"Janie Runaway"	Steely Dan	2000
"When Sinatra Played Juarez"	Tom Russell	2001
"The Singer"	Rosemary Clooney	2001

Works Cited

Ackelson, Richard W. *Frank Sinatra: A Complete Recording History.* Jefferson, NC: McFarland, 1992.

Adamowski, T.H. "Love in the Western World: Sinatra and the Conflict of Generations." *Frank Sinatra and Popular Culture: Essays on an American Icon.* Ed. Leonard Mustazza. Westport, CT: Praeger Press, 1998. 26–37.

Austin, Norman. *Archery at the Dark of the Moon: Poetic Problems in Homer's Odyssey.* Berkeley: University of California Press, 1975.

Baker, William. "Bernard Kops." *British Playwrights 1956–1995: A Research and Production Sourcebook.* Ed. William Demastes. Westport, CT: Greenwood Press, 1995, 227–236.

Barrow, R.H. *The Romans.* Middlesex, England: Penguin Books, 1949.

Brackett, David. *Interpreting Popular Music.* Cambridge, MA: Cambridge University Press, 1995.

Cahn, Sammy. *I Should Care: The Sammy Cahn Story.* New York: Arbor House, 1974.

———. *Sammy Cahn Songbook.* Secaucus, NJ: Warner Brothers Publications Inc., 1986.

Cahn, Sammy, and James Van Heusen. "Notes." *Only the Lonely.* Capitol Records, 1958.

Campbell, Tom. *Las Vegas.* Port Washington, NY: Skyline Press, 1984.

Clayton-Lea, Tony. *Elvis Costello: A Biography.* New York: Fromm International, 1998.

Cooper, B. Lee. *Images of American Society in Popular Music: A Guide to Reflective Teaching.* Chicago: Nelson-Hall, 1982.

Cornyn, Stan. "After All These Years." *Francis A. and Edward K.* Reprise Records, 1968.

———. " 'The Anchovy Tonight Is an Endangered Species.' " *L.A. Is My Lady.* Qwest Records, 1984.

———. "At Last." *Francis Albert Sinatra and Antonio Carlos Jobim.* Reprise Records, 1967.

———. "A Conversation with Mr. Jones." *It Might as Well Be Swing.* Reprise Records, 1964.

———. "Eye Witness." *FAS: Frank Sinatra—The Complete Reprise Studio Recordings.* Reprise Records, 1995.

———. "Francis Albert Sinatra (b. 12 December 1915, Hoboken, N.J.)." *Sinatra: A Man and His Music.* Reprise Records, 1965.

———. "Frank Sinatra Sings All There Is to Know about Love." *Softly as I Leave You.* Reprise Records, 1964.

———. "Frank Sinatra Sings of Days and Loves Ago." *September of My Years.* Reprise Records, 1965.

———. "Frank Sinatra Sings the Greatest Songs from Musical Comedy: An Interview with Sonny Burke." *My Kind of Broadway.* Reprise Records, 1965.

———. "My, My." *That's Life.* Reprise Records, 1966.

———. "On Sinatra or How to Be Timeless Tonight." *Strangers in the Night.* Reprise Records, 1966.

———. "Sinatra at the Sands." *Sinatra at the Sands with Count Basie and the Orchestra.* Reprise Records, 1966.

———. "The Singer Today: An Interview with Jimmy Bowen." *Sinatra '65.* Reprise Records, 1965.

———. Untitled. *Frank Sinatra: The World We Knew.* Reprise Records, 1967.

———. Untitled. *Moonlight Sinatra.* Reprise Records, 1966.

———. Untitled. *My Way.* Reprise Records, 1969.

———. Untitled. *Ol' Blue Eyes Is Back.* Reprise Records, 1973.

DeLillo, Dan. *Underworld.* New York: Scribner, 1997.

De Mattia, Sally. "A Personal Testimony and a View from Europe: The Multicultural Frank Sinatra." *Voices in Italian Americana* 10.2 (1999): 54–62.

Doctorow, E.L. *City of God.* New York: Random House, 2000.

Early, Gerald. "Listening to Frank Sinatra." Prairie Schooner 63.3 (Fall 1989): 108–110.

Fericano, Paul. "SINATRA, SINATRA: The Poem." Millbrae, CA: Poor Souls Press/Scaramouche Books, 1982.

Fokkelman, J.P. "Exodus." *The Literary Guide to the Bible*. Ed. Robert Alter and Frank Kermode. Cambridge, MA: The Belknap Press, 1987, 56–65.

Freedland, Michael. *All the Way: A Biography of Frank Sinatra*. New York: St. Martin's Press, 1997.

Friedwald, Will. *Sinatra—The Song is You: The Singer's Art*. New York: Scribner, 1995.

———. "Songs for Swingin' Singles: An Appreciation." *Frank Sinatra: The Complete Capitol Singles Collection*. Capitol Records, 1996.

Frith, Simon, and Andrew Goodwin, eds. *On Record: Rock, Pop, and the Written Word*. New York: Pantheon Books, 1990.

Gilbert, Roger. "The Swinger and the Loser: Sinatra, Masculinity, and 50s Culture." *Epoch* 48 (1999): 144–157.

Ginsberg, Allen. *Collected Poems 1947–1980*. New York: Perennial Library, 1988.

Gleason, Ralph. "Frank: Then and Now." *The Frank Sinatra Reader*. Ed. Steven Petkov and Leonard Mustazza. New York: Oxford University Press, 1995, 225–227.

———. "Notes by Ralph J. Gleason." *No One Cares*. Capitol Records, 1959.

Gouldstone, David. *Elvis Costello: God's Comic*. New York: St. Martin's Press, 1989.

Hamill, Peter. *Why Sinatra Matters*. Boston: Little, Brown, and Company, 1998.

Hazuka, Tom. *In the City of the Disappeared*. Bridgehampton, NY: Bridge Works Publishing, 2000.

Hegner, William. *King Corso*. New York: Pocket Books, 1973.

Hemming, Roy, and David Hajdu. *Discovering Great Singers of Classic Pop*. New York: Newmarket Press, 1991.

Holder, Deborah. *Completely Frank: The Life of Frank Sinatra*. London: Bloomsbury Publishing, 1995.

Jacobs, Dick. *Who Wrote That Song?* White Hall, VA: Betterway Publications, Inc., 1988.

Kaplan, Mike, ed. *Variety Presents the Complete Book of Major U.S. Show Business Awards*. New York: Garland, 1985.

Kashner, Sam. "The Loneliest Guy in the World." *GQ: Gentleman's Quarterly* (November 1999): 341–358.

———. *Sinatraland*. Woodstock, NY: Overlook Press, 1999.

King, Alan. *Name Dropping: The Life and Lies of Alan King*. New York: Touchstone, 1996.

Kolodny, Annette. *The Land Before Her: Fantasy and Experience of the American Frontiers, 1630–1860*. Chapel Hill: University of North Carolina Press, 1984.

Kops, Bernard. *Playing Sinatra*. London: Samuel French, 1992.

Kuntz, Tom, and Phil Kuntz, eds. *The Sinatra Files: The Secret FBI Dossier*. New York: Three Rivers Press, 2000.

Kutler, Stanley I., ed. *The Encyclopedia of the Vietnam War*. New York: Charles Scribner's Sons, 1996.

Lahr, John. *Sinatra: The Artist and the Man*. New York: Random House, 1997.

Lanham, Richard. *A Handlist of Rhetorical Terms*. 2nd edition. Berkeley: University of California Press, 1991.

Lees, Gene. "Frank Sinatra: Confessions and Contradictions." *The Frank Sinatra Reader*. Ed. Steven Petkov and Leonard Mustazza. New York: Oxford University Press, 1995. 139–142.

Lloyd, David. "The Heavens." *Denver Quarterly* 34.1 (1999): 32.

Lonstein, Albert L., and Vito R. Marino. *The Revised Compleat Sinatra*. Ellenville, NY: Sondra M. Lonstein, 1979.

Marino, Vito R., and Anthony C. Furfeo. *The Official Price Guide to Frank Sinatra Records and CDs*. New York: House of Collectibles, 1993.

Modic, William D. " 'Boys' Night Out': The Evolution of the Rat Pack in a Changing Hollywood." Delivered at the Annual Conference of the Northeast Popular Culture Association. Quinnipiac College, Hamden, CT, November 1996.

Morris, Charles. *Signs, Language, and Behavior*. New York: Prentice Hall, 1946.

Mustazza, Leonard, ed. *Frank Sinatra and Popular Culture: Essays on an American Icon*. Westport, CT: Praeger Press, 1998.

———. *The Frank Sinatra Encyclopedia*. Westport, CT: Greenwood Press, 1998.

Nelson, Michael. "Frank Sinatra: The Loneliness of the Long Distance Singer." *VQR: The Virginia Quarterly Review* 75 (Autumn 1999): 605–621.

Newman, Randy. "On the Records." *Guilty: Thirty Years of Randy Newman*. Rhino Records, 1998. 47–65.

Nuñez, Raul. *The Lonely Hearts Club*. Trans. by Ed Emery. London: Serpent's Tail, 1989.

O'Brien, Ed, and Scott P. Sayers, Jr. *Sinatra: The Man and His Music—The Recording Artistry of Francis Albert Sinatra, 1939–1992*. Austin: TDS Publishers, 1992.

Pattison, Robert. *The Triumph of Vulgarity: Rock Music in the Mirror of Romanticism*. New York: Oxford University Press, 1987.

Pleasants, Henry. *The Great American Popular Singers: The Lives, Careers, and Art*. New York: Simon and Schuster, 1974.

Rockwell, John. *Sinatra: An American Classic*. New York: Rolling Stone Press, 1984.

Santurri, Edmund. "Theology and Music in a Different Key: Meditations on Frank Sinatra and *Eros* in a Fallen World." From *Sinatra and Popular Culture: Essays on an American Icon*. Ed. Leonard Mustazza. Westport, CT: Praeger Press, 1998. 198–210.

Scholes, Robert. *Protocols of Reading.* New Haven: Yale University Press, 1989.

Schudson, Michael. *Advertising: The Uneasy Persuasion.* New York: Basic Books, 1984.

Shaw, Arnold. *Sinatra: Twentieth-Century Romantic.* New York: Holt, Rinehart, and Winston, 1968.

Shirak, Ed, Jr. *Our Way (Based on the Song "A Time That Was").* Hoboken, NJ: Lepore's Publishing, 1995.

Shurley, Neil. "Commandments." *Rosebud* 3.3 (1996): 60–62.

Silva, Luiz Carlos do Nascimento. *Put Your Dreams Away: A Frank Sinatra Discography.* Westport, CT: Greenwood Press, 2000.

Simon, George. *The Big Bands.* New York: Macmillan Company, 1967.

Sinatra, Frank. "The Playboy Interview." *Playboy* 10.2 (1963): 35–36, 38–40.

———. "What's This about Races?" *Frank Sinatra and Popular Culture: Essays on an American Icon.* Ed. Leonard Mustazza. Westport, CT: Praeger Press, 1998. 23–25.

Sinatra, Nancy. *Frank Sinatra, an American Legend.* Santa Monica: General Publishing Group, 1995.

Sinatra, Tina. *My Father's Daughter: A Memoir.* New York: Simon and Schuster, 2000.

Talese, Gay. "Frank Sinatra Has a Cold." *The Frank Sinatra Reader.* Ed. Steven Petkov and Leonard Mustazza. New York: Oxford University Press, 1995, 99–129.

———. "Sinatra Means a Jumping Jilly's and a Lot Less Sleep for Another Cat at His Favorite Bar." *Legend: Frank Sinatra and the American Dream.* Ed. Ethlie Ann Vare. New York: Boulevard Books, 1988.

Taraborrelli, J. Randy. *Sinatra: A Complete Life.* Secaucus, NJ: Birch Lane Press, 1997.

Tharp, Twyla. *When Push Comes to Shove.* New York: Linda Gray Bantam Books, 1992.

Tollin, Anthony. "The Programs." *60 Greatest Old-Time Radio Shows Starring Frank Sinatra and Friends.* Radio Spirits, Inc., 2000, 6–62.

Trudeau, Garry. *That's Doctor Sinatra, You Little Bimbo.* New York: Henry Holt and Company, 1986.

Vare, Ethlie Ann, ed. *Legend: Frank Sinatra and the American Dream.* New York: Boulevard Books, 1995.

Ventura, Michael. *The Death of Frank Sinatra.* New York: St. Martin's Press, 1997.

Whitman, Walt. *Leaves of Grass. The First (1855) Edition.* Ed. Malcolm Cowley. New York: The Viking Press, 1959.

Wicke, Jennifer. *Advertising Fictions: Literature, Advertisement, and Social Reading.* New York: Columbia University Press, 1988.

Wiener, Jon. "When Old Blue Eyes Was Red." *Legend: Frank Sinatra and the American Dream*. Ed. Ethlie Ann Vare. New York: Boulevard Books, 1995. 64–69.

Wilson, Earl. *Sinatra: An Unauthorized Biography*. New York: Macmillan Publishing Company, 1976.

Wolfe, Tom. "The Birth of 'The New Journalism'; Eyewitness Report by Tom Wolfe." *New York* 5.7 (February 14, 1972): cover, 30–38, 43–45.

Zangrillo, Vincent. "Saint Francis." *Voices in Italian Americana* 10.2 (1999): 74–76.

Zehme, Bill. *The Way You Wear Your Hat: Frank Sinatra and the Lost Art of Livin'*. New York: HarperCollins, 1997.

Index

About the Author

GILBERT L. GIGLIOTTI is Associate Professor and Assistant Chairman in the Department of English at Central Connecticut State University, where he teaches an annual course in the literature of Sinatra. He also hosts a weekly Sinatra program on the campus radio station and is frequently invited to speak about the singer by local organizations.